Church PLANT Manual

Church PLANT Manual

Edited by Rev. Ted Smith

World Impact Press
3701 East 13th Street North
Suite 100
Wichita, Kansas 67208

Church PLANT Manual

© 2024. World Impact, Inc. All Rights Reserved. Copying, redistribution, and/or sale of these materials, or any unauthorized transmission, except as may be expressly permitted by the 1976 Copyright Act or in writing from the publisher is prohibited. Requests for permission should be addressed in writing to:

    World Impact
    3701 East 13th Street North
    Suite 100
    Wichita, KS 67208

ISBN: 978-1-62932-081-6

Published by World Impact Press

All Scripture quotations, unless otherwise noted, are from The Holy Bible, English Standard Version, © 2001 by Crossway Bible, a division of Good News Publishers. Used by permission. All Rights Reserved.

This book is dedicated to Dr. Don Davis, without whom this resource would not be possible. His prophetic voice, prolific writing on the subject, leadership development training materials, and consistent clarion call to Christians everywhere to engage in the work of Christ that a throng of healthy churches would be planted across the United States and around the world inspires every word you will read in this brief volume.

Dr. Davis's work in the fields of theology, biblical studies, and urban church planting serves as the firm foundation upon which this text stands. To say we are indebted to Dr. Davis would be an absurd understatement.

Careful readers will note as they navigate this work that we quote largely from and have indeed imported much of his teachings in this text. We pray that this resource honors his tremendous legacy and that indeed a multitude of healthy churches, who will raise the banner of Christ Jesus in communities impacted by poverty, will arise that the world might know the love of God expressed in Christ and come to saving faith in the Nazarene.

May his clarion call be heard by all who engage with this text. May that call point us to Jesus, inspire our church planting efforts, and advance the Kingdom of our Christ for His glory.

– Rev. Ted Smith

TABLE OF CONTENTS

Foreword xi

Preface xv

Acknowledgments xix

Introduction 1
   Biblical Foundations for Church Planting 3
   Pauline Precedents from Acts: The Pauline Cycle . . . 5
   Church Planting Overview 7

Session 1: Prepare 13
   Seminar 1
   Charting Your Course 15
   Seminar 2
   Building Your Team 18
   Seminar 3
   Building Resilience 23

Team Exercises: Prepare 27
   Exercise 1
   Establishing Context 29
   Exercise 2
   Defining Values and Vision 31
   Exercise 3
   Team Effectiveness 33
   Exercise 4
   Building Resilience 35

Session 2: Launch and Assemble 37
Seminar 4
The Driving Force of the Gospel 39
Seminar 5
Navigating Culture and Context 45
Seminar 6
Evangelism and Follow-Up 49

Team Exercises: Launch and Assemble 57
Exercise 5
The Driving Force of the Gospel 59
Exercise 6
Navigating Culture and Context 61
Exercise 7
Evangelism and Follow-up 63

Session 3: Nurture and Transition (Multiplication) . . 65
Seminar 7
Effective Discipling 67
Seminar 8
Leadership Development 71
Seminar 9
Creating Pathways for Multiplication 77

Team Exercises: Nurture and Transition 83
Exercise 8
Nurture: Mature the Church 85
Exercise 9
Transition: Multiplication Strategy 87

Session 4: Bringing It All Together 89

Seminar 10
Using Wisdom in Ministry 91

Seminar 11
Creating Your Strategy 101

Seminar 12
Adapt to Win 105

Team Exercises: Bringing It All Together 111

Exercise 10
Creating a Church Planting Calendar 113

Exercise 11
Completing Your Evangel Charter 116

Exercise Supplement
Sample Evangel Charter 118

Afterword 121

Foreword

I Will Build My Church

People aren't saved just to go to heaven. God is creating a people. We can't lose sight of this. Unfortunately, too many have reduced the salvation story to a simple formula of "God made the world, we are sinners, so God sent Jesus to save each of us from our sins." Creation, sin, Jesus, and that's a wrap!

Some wonder, well, what's wrong with that? Here's what's wrong: the creation-sin-Jesus formula leads to a hyper-individualized Christianity, with our faith being exclusively about our personal lives. Jesus becomes an ecclesiastical bellhop to serve me, myself, and I. We cheapen the gospel message to crass consumption.

The Bible provides an in-depth story, not a simple formula. When we confess Jesus Christ, we are confessing the world-changing idea that Christ came to die for sins, defeat Satan and destroy his works, and reestablish the reign of God in the earth. That's the work Jesus did with his life, death, burial, and resurrection. From the book of Acts on, the New Testament is written under the assumption that you are living in community with others within the confines of a local church. Salvation is personal but it's to be lived out communally.

What makes the church different from all other societal institutions? The holiness factor. Holiness is the way to victory. It's the empowering ingredient that destroys sin and makes room for transformation. It's what makes us God's people. Our faith in Christ provides access to this. The same power that raised Jesus from the dead is the source for renovating lives and communities.

The first twelve chapters of Acts tells the story of the formation of the church. The first key figure is Peter. This should come as no surprise, as when Peter confessed his belief that Jesus was God's son, Jesus told him that he would be a key church planter (Matt. 16:18).

After the resurrection, Christ invested forty days into his followers. During this time, the power source of the Holy Spirit was revealed. Jesus taught about the Kingdom of God and that all believers are to live as citizens of it. What made it possible was the presence of the Holy Spirit. He taught them that the Kingdom would not come until he returned a second time to defeat evil once and for all. Until then, all his followers are to work to expand God's Kingdom, and the vehicle to do that is the local church.

Alvin Sanders
President and CEO, World Impact
March 28, 2024

A Word from the Director of Church Planting

The meta-narrative of the cosmos is the reality of two kingdoms in conflict. The Kingdom of God has won the victory through its Champion, Jesus of Nazareth. Through the incarnation, crucifixion, and His resurrection, Jesus has, "stripped all the spiritual tyrants in the universe of their sham authority at the Cross and marched them naked through the streets" (Col. 2:15, *The Message*).

Though the kingdom of darkness has been defeated, Satan and his minions keep billions of souls trapped in spiritual bondage. Not desiring that any should perish, but that all should be set free by the power of the gospel, Jesus gave a mission charge to His Church, to get up, get out and to move forward and multiply. This is the essential task of the Church – Missions – the sending of authorized (identified, equipped, commissioned) individuals to go into unchurched communities to proclaim the Gospel, win converts, make disciples of the converts, and gather them together to form functioning, multiplying churches that will bear the fruit of the Kingdom of God in that community.

This *Church PLANT Manual* is the equipping resource used to coach church plant teams in the foundational principles of planting healthy churches in communities experiencing poverty, here and around the world.

The Lord will return soon, and His reward will be with Him. Until then, let's not shrink back from our essential task of identifying, equipping, and commissioning laborers to bring good news leading to new churches being planted.

". . . not of those who shrink back . . ." (Heb. 10:39)

Rev. Bob Engel
Director of Church Planting
March 28, 2024

Preface

Planting churches in places where the name of Jesus is not yet known or worshiped is both a profound calling and an integral part of the Christian mission. This mission resonates deeply with the heartbeat of biblical theology, which emphasizes God's call for the world's peoples to know him and his kingdom reign through His Son, Jesus Christ of Nazareth. Even a little reflection provides compelling reasons for this noble and still pertinent pursuit in today's confused and broken world.

Church Planting Employs the Apostolic Method to Fulfill the Great Commission

Jesus's final charge to His disciples, known as the Great Commission (Matt. 28:18-20), commands them to "go and make disciples of all nations." This mandate extends to personal evangelism within familiar or already-reached contexts and extends to all geographic and cultural boundaries. Those neighborhoods that have neither heard nor responded to God's offer of redemption and salvation must hear the Good News in a way that they can understand and accept. Planting churches in areas where Christ is unknown embodies this call, ensuring that every people group has the opportunity to encounter the Gospel. Through the local church, discipleship and baptism can occur, laying a foundational community for new believers to grow in their faith.

Church Planting Acknowledges the Local Church as the Kingdom's Locus and Agent

The narrative of Scripture unfolds the theme of God's kingdom rule expanding across the earth, from the covenant promise to Abraham that all peoples on earth would be blessed through him (Gen. 12:1-3) to the vision in Revelation of a multitude from every nation, tribe, people, and language worshiping before the throne of God (Rev. 7:9-10). Church planting is the apostolic activity that serves as a tangible expression of this kingdom expansion. To plant a local church where Christ is known and glorified demonstrates where God's rule and reign are manifest (locus) and where that reign can be demonstrated and announced in new neighborhoods among new groups of people (agent).

Church Planting Represents a Tangible Demonstration of God's Love for People Yet to Believe

The lovingkindness of the Almighty God for the world through his Son Jesus Christ is the dominant message of the New Testament. John 3:16 powerfully summarizes and declares this elemental claim, announcing God's love revealed in the sacrificial sending of His Son for all humanity. Planting churches is a tangible act revealing this love, communicating to every neighborhood, person, and group that his offer extends to all. No place is too remote, different, or challenging for the Gospel; all places everywhere deserve to hear of God's sovereign plan to save a remnant of humankind for his eternal purpose. Every new church planting effort is visible proof of the inclusivity of God's invitation to salvation; that new gathering of believers both underscores and affirms the worth and value of every person and every soul in that community regarding God's eternal plan.

Church Planting is the Divine Catalyst for Social and Cultural Transformation

Finally, when the Good News of Christ comes alive within a community, the local assembly, through the Holy Spirit, becomes a powerful agent of transformation, spiritually, socially, and culturally. Churches become witnessing centers of hope, offering practical expressions of love through justice, education, healthcare, and community development. They address not only the spiritual vacuum of life without a true knowledge of God through Christ but also the physical and societal needs of the community. By planting churches in areas unfamiliar with the Gospel, Christians can initiate holistic transformation, reflecting the Kingdom of God in its fullness.

In conclusion, as you engage in the apostolic call to plant churches in neighborhoods where Jesus is not yet known, you reenact God's mission. Church planting resonates with the core of the Church's calling and practically reveals the heart of God. It embodies the Great Commission, expands the manifestation of God's Kingdom, communicates God's love for all peoples, and catalyzes comprehensive transformation practically where kingdom life must be shown. This mission fulfills a biblical mandate and aligns with the most profound expressions of Christian faith and practice, making it a compelling and urgent pursuit for the church today.

Our sincere prayer is that the Lord Jesus accompany you as you establish your unique local outpost of the Kingdom of God, the local church, in the community where you serve and minister! He will accompany you along the Way.

Dr. Don Davis
Senior Executive Advisor to the President
March 28, 2024

Acknowledgments

I would like to acknowledge and express my gratitude to a host of World Impact staff whose prayer, time, reflection, and efforts in the production, review, and support of this resource cannot be fully captured in words. You will never know their names but their commitment to Christ and work on your behalf to provide this resource speak for themselves.

I would especially like to acknowledge Rev. Bob Engel, Rev. Luke Raughley, Rev. Jordan King, Pastor Lorenzo Elizondo, and Pastor David Estrada for their time, dedication, and prayerful efforts to produce this text. Without their faithful friendship, partnership, tireless work, and constant encouragement this work would have never moved beyond a dream.

As this training will evidence, we believe in teams. I have been blessed of the Lord to work with several teams who have invested much to produce a resource that we pray will serve you well as you PLANT the church the Lord has birthed in your hearts.

Rev. Ted Smith
Dean of Church Plant Schools
March 28, 2024

INTRODUCTION

Rev. Ted Smith

The *Church PLANT Manual* was designed to help your church plant team understand the principles of church planting, navigate the journey of turning those principles into actionable goals during coaching sessions of an Evangel School, and ultimately to develop your team's strategic plan for the next twelve months of your church.

The guidebook and the Evangel School itself are intended for those who are planting a new church, those who are preparing to re-plant (restart, revitalize, or relaunch) an existing church, those who are seeking a process for transitioning into the next generation of pastoral leadership, and those seeking to catalyze a church planting movement.

Evangel is a principle-based strategy which can be applied to multiply contexts of planting, re-planting, seasons of transition, and other applications. This has been proven through the years as we have coached teams to develop a strategy for their unique context. Therefore, it is important to note that the terms "plant" and "planting" should always be understood as inclusive terms related to the PLANT principles of Evangel.

As no guidebook alone is fully sufficient to prepare and assist a church plant team in their work, in addition to this resource, all church plant teams will receive and be led by an Evangel Coach during an Evangel School as they complete team exercises and discern their unique path with their team. Beyond the Evangel School, each church plant team who completes the school and charters with World Impact will be provided an Evangel Field Coach who will walk with the team for twelve months after the school as they seek to plant the church God has birthed in their hearts for His glory.

Biblical Foundations for Church Planting
Rev. Ted Smith

The Scripture is clear that the Lord would build His church (Matt. 16:18) often referred to as the "Church Universal"[1] and that the Lord Himself is "the head of the body, the church" (Col. 1:18). Therefore, all church planting efforts rest squarely on the authority and command of Christ to "Go therefore and make disciples of all nations, baptizing them in the name of the Father and of the Son and of the Holy Spirit, teaching them to observe all that I have commanded you. And behold, I am with you always, to the end of the age" (Matt. 28:19-20). And yet, many who endeavor to plant churches today will hear a familiar retort, "Why do we need another church? There is a church on every corner in America." Hyperbole aside, there are many churches across our nation.

Why Would We Need More Churches?

The devil's influence "in the world" (since the fall, Gen. 3:1-15) is evident in Scripture. Jesus referred to him as "the prince (ruler) of this world" (John 12:31). Paul called him "the ruler of the air… spirit at work in the disobedient" (Eph. 2:2) and the "god of this age (world)" (2 Cor. 4:4). John wrote that, "the whole world is under the control of the evil one" (1 John 5:19).

To be clear, the devil is not God's equal. He is not all powerful and certainly no match for Jesus.

There will be a final judgment and a decisive victory over Satan. He will be "thrown into the lake of fire" and "tormented forever" (Rev. 20:10). Any kingdom and/or authority will be taken away from Satan. All will be given back to King Jesus, its rightful

---

1   From the Latin *Ecclesia Universalis* referring to the Church throughout the world.

Author and Owner. In the meantime, people live out their days in either the world or the church. The world is influenced (controlled) by Satan. By contrast, the Church is influenced (controlled) by the Holy Spirit. This is the key to our understanding of and need for the church.

Two texts in Ephesians 2:12-22 and Ephesians 3:10-21 are helpful in our considerations. These texts unpack two answers to the question, "Why do we need more churches?" First, it is clear from these texts that God works in the church (among His people). Another way of saying this is that the church is the "locus" (location, place, and/or context) of God's salvation, of the empowering presence of the Holy Spirit, and the authentic expression of the Kingdom's life and witness. His desire is to form a new humanity in the church. Second, these texts bear out that God works through the church (through His people). Another way to express this truth is to say, the church is the "agent" of God, a willing and available servant to God to advance kingdom purposes in the world." Through the church God reconciles the world to Himself.[2]

The biblical truth is that the local church is the only hope for people caught up in the enemy's attacks, enslavement, distractions, and schemes. Though his influence is everywhere, the church stands as God's locus and agent offering people the opportunity to find freedom in this dark world. Praise God, that Jesus came "to destroy the works of the devil" (1 John 3:8).

---

[2] For a deeper discussion of the church as "locus" and "agent" see the seminar "Theology of the Church for Team Leaders" in *The Timothy Conference Workbook*, Wichita: TUMI Press, 2005, pp. 39-46.

Pauline Precedents from Acts: The Pauline Cycle[3]

World Impact, as a missions organization, has rooted our church planting efforts in the missionary activity of the Apostle Paul, and his missionary team, in establishing new churches as laid out in the book of Acts. The following outline is helpful for those exploring a strategy for church planting.

1. Missionaries Commissioned: *Acts 13:1-4; 15:39-40; Gal. 1:15-16*

2. Audience Contacted: *Acts 13:14-16; 14:1; 16:13-15; 17:16-19*

3. Gospel Communicated: *Acts 13:17-41; 16:31; Rom. 10:9-14; 2 Tim. 2:8*

4. Hearers Converted: *Acts. 13:48; 16:14-15; 20:21; 26:20; 1 Thess. 1:9-10*

5. Believers Congregated: *Acts 13:43; 19:9; Rom. 16:4-5; 1 Cor. 14:26*

6. Faith Confirmed: *Acts 14:21-22; 15:41; Rom. 16:17; Col. 1:28; 2 Thess. 2:15; 1 Tim. 1:3*

7. Leadership Consecrated: *Acts 14:23; 2 Tim. 2:2; Titus 1:5*

8. Believers Commended: *Acts 14:23; 16:40; 21:32 (2 Tim. 4:9 and Titus 3:12 by implication)*

9. Relationships Continued: *Acts 15:36; 18:23; 1 Cor. 16:5; Eph. 6:21-22; Col. 4:7-8*

10. Sending Churches Convened: *Acts 14:26-27; 15:1-4*

---

3 The "Pauline Cycle" terminology, stages, and diagram are taken from David J. Hesselgrave, *Planting Churches Cross-Culturally*, 2nd ed. Grand Rapids: Baker Book House, 2000. "Evangelize, Equip, and Empower" and "PLANT" schemas for church planting taken from *Crowns of Beauty: Planting Urban Churches Conference Binder*, Los Angeles: World Impact Press, 1999 and *Ripe for Harvest: A Guidebook for Planting Healthy Churches in the City*, Wichita: TUMI Press, 2016, p. 61.

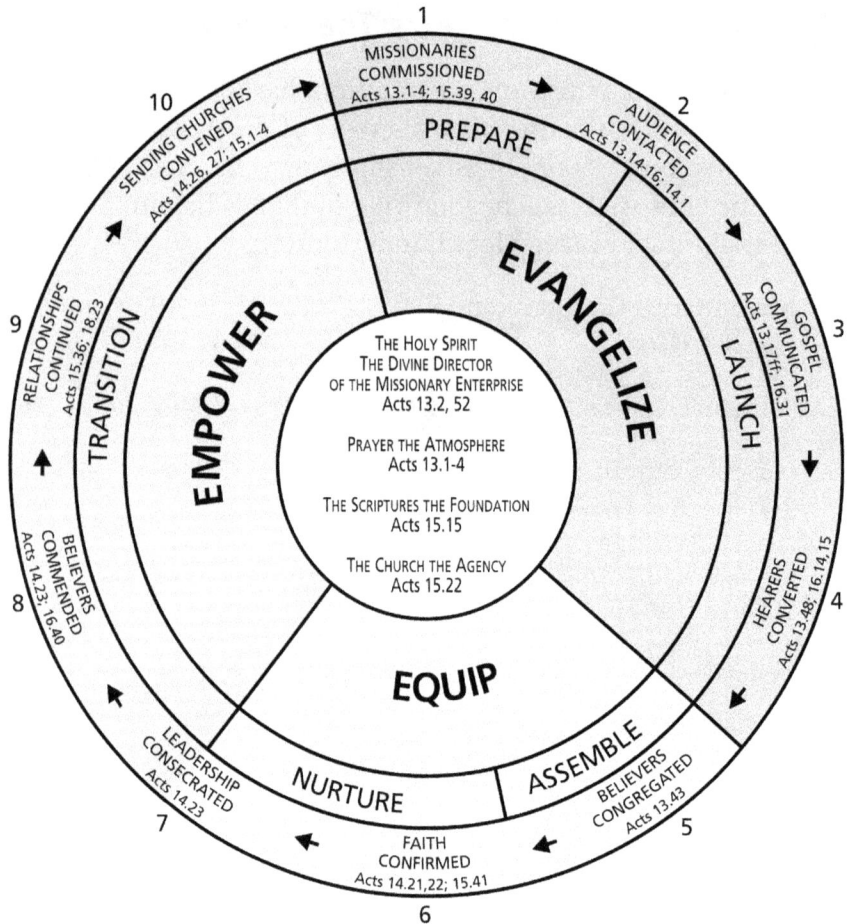

From this outline, World Impact developed a the three-fold missionary approach of Evangelism, Equipping, and Empowerment in our efforts to reach new communities with the gospel, make disciples, and in time release ministries to local leaders. The PLANT strategy was born from this approach and gave birth to the Evangel School of Urban Church Planting material and training.

Church Planting Overview[4]

How to PLANT a Church

EVANGELIZE

Prepare: Be the Church
Principle: A church is birthed from an existing church.

- Pray.
- Form a church plant team.
- Select a target area and population.
- Conduct demographic and cultural studies.

Launch: Expand the Church
Principle: Begin inviting people to join the community.

- Recruit and train additional volunteers.
- Conduct evangelistic events.

EQUIP

Assemble: Establish the Church
Principle: Bring the church to a place where it can be announced in the community.

- Form cell groups, Bible studies, etc.
- Follow up with new believers.
- Identify and train emerging leaders.
- Promote the new church to the neighborhood.

Nurture: Mature the Church
Principle: Leaders develop and practice their developing gifts under the oversight of pastoral leadership.

- Develop individual and group discipleship.
- Identify and use spiritual gifts and fill key roles in the church.

EMPOWER

Transition: Multiply the Church
Principle: Raise up leaders to take over the church plant or send teams to plant daughter churches.

- Develop a multiplication strategy.
- Partner with other urban churches for fellowship, support, and mission.

---

[4] Adapted from a seminar by Rev. Dr. Don L. Davis in *Ripe for Harvest,* pp. 54-60.

Ten Principles of Church Planting[5]

1. *Jesus is Lord.* (Matt. 9:37-38) All church plant activity is made effective and fruitful under the watch care and power of the Lord Jesus, who himself is the Lord of the harvest.

2. *Evangelize, Equip, and Empower unreached people to reach people.* (1 Thess. 1:6-8) Our goal in reaching others for Christ is not only for solid conversion but also for dynamic multiplication; those who are reached must be trained to reach others as well.

3. *Be inclusive: whosoever will may come.* (Rom. 10:12) No strategy should forbid any person or group from entering into the Kingdom through Jesus Christ by faith.

4. *Be culturally neutral: Come just as you are.* (Col. 3:11) The Gospel places no demands on any seeker to change their culture as a prerequisite for coming to Jesus; they may come just as they are.

5. *Avoid a fortress mentality.* (Acts 1:8) The goal of missions is not to create an impregnable castle in the midst of an unsaved community, but a dynamic outpost of the Kingdom which launches a witness for Jesus within and unto the very borders of their world.

6. *Continue to evangelize to avoid stagnation.* (Rom. 1:16-17) Keep looking to the horizons with the vision of the Great Commission in mind; foster an environment of aggressive witness for Christ.

7. *Cross racial, class, gender, and language barriers.* (1 Cor. 9:19-22) Use your freedom in Christ to find new, credible ways to communicate the kingdom message to those farthest from the cultural spectrum of the traditional church.

---

5   *Mere Missions*, Wichita: TUMI Press, 2022. pp 234-236.

8. ***Respect the dominance of the receiving culture.*** (Acts 15:23-29) Allow the Holy Spirit to incarnate the vision and the ethics of the Kingdom of God in the words, language, customs, styles, and experience of those who have embraced Jesus as their Lord.

9. ***Avoid dependence.*** (Eph. 4:11-16) Neither patronize nor be overly stingy towards the growing congregation; do not underestimate the power of the Spirit in the midst of even the smallest Christian community to accomplish God's work in their community.

10. ***Think reproducibility.*** (2 Tim. 2:2; Phil. 1:18) In every activity and project you initiate, think in terms of equipping others to do the same by maintaining an open mind regarding the means and ends of your missionary endeavors.

Overview of Church Plant Planning Phases[6]

Rev. Dr. Don L. Davis

	Prepare	Launch
Definition	Forming a team of called members who ready themselves to plant a church under the Holy Spirit's direction	Penetrating the selected community by conducting evangelistic events among the target population
Purpose	Seek God regarding the target population and community, the formation of your church plant team, organizing strategic intercession for the community, and doing research on its needs and opportunities	Mobilize team and recruit volunteers to conduct ongoing evangelistic events and holistic outreach to win associates and neighbors to Christ
Parent-Child Metaphor	Decision and Conception	Pre-natal Care
Question Focus During Dialogue	Questions about: • Preparing your team • The target community • Strategic prayer initiatives • Demographic studies	Questions about: • Character and number of evangelistic events • Communication and advertisement of events • Recruiting and coordinating volunteers • Identity and name of the outreach
Cardinal Virtue	Openness to the Lord	Courage to engage the community
Critical Vices	Presumption and "paralysis of analysis"	Intimidation and haughtiness
Bottom Line	Cultivate a period of listening and reflecting	Initiate your engagement with boldness and confidence

---

6 *Mere Missions*, pp. 248-249

Assemble	Nurture	Transition
Gathering the cells of converts together to form a local assembly of believers, announcing the new church to the neighbors in the community	Nurturing member and leadership discipleship, enabling members to function in their spiritual gifts, and establishing solid infrastructure within the Christian assembly	Empowering the church for independence by equipping leaders for autonomy, transferring authority, and creating structures for financial independence
Form cell groups, Bible studies, or home fellowships for follow-up, continued evangelism, and ongoing growth toward public birth of the church	Develop individual and group discipleship by filling key roles in the body based on burden and gifting of members	Commission members and elders, install pastor, and foster church associations
Childbirth	Growth and Parenting	Maturity to Adulthood
Questions about: • Follow-up and incorporation of new believers • Make-up of small group life • The character of public worship • Initial church structures and procedures • Initial body life and growth • Cultural friendliness of church	Questions about: • Discipling individuals and leaders • Helping members identify gifts and burdens (teams) • Credentials for leadership • Church order, government, and discipline	Questions about: • Incorporation • Affiliations and associations • Transferring leadership • Missionary transition • Ongoing reproduction
Wisdom to discern God's timing	Focus upon the faithful core	Dependence on the Spirit's ability
Impatience and cowardice	Neglect and micromanagement	Paternalism and quick release
Celebrate the announcement of your body with joy	Concentrate on investing in the faithful	Pass the baton with confidence in the Spirit's continued working

PLANT

Session 1: Prepare

In this session, we will discuss the importance of contextualizing the principles of Evangel for your church planting efforts, building an effective church plant team, and building resilience for church planting.

Seminar 1
Charting Your Course

Seminar 2
Building Your Team

Seminar 3
Building Resilience

Seminar 1
Charting Your Course
Rev. Ted Smith

It is important that your team filter the PLANT principles of the Evangel School through the lens of the context of the community your church will serve.

I. Determine Your Context.

Each team the Lord calls will possess a different vision for the church and will approach church planting efforts in various ways. Whether you are planting a church in your own culture or planting a church cross-culturally, you will need to chart your own unique journey, being informed by the principles presented in Evangel.

Seminars, questions, and team exercises are provided that will prompt your team to consider issues relevant to your unique church planting context. You should spend much time reflecting on the issues of the community where you will PLANT using the questions covered in each team exercise to get the maximum benefit from the material and the time investment of your team.

II. Determine Your Vision.

To thrive in your efforts, church planters must adopt a clear theological vision and choose sound, culturally sensitive models, and expressions of the church. You must apply biblical wisdom to effectively evangelize, equip, and empower people to respond to the love of Christ and take their place in representing Christ's Kingdom where they live and work.[1]

---

1 *Ripe for Harvest*, p. 11.

In every activity, big and small, your church plant team must have a clear sense of your collective vision and your personal contribution to that vision.[2]

A clear vision will help you separate the statements "We can do it" from "We should do it" and will keep you from basing decisions on emotion, expediency, or available resources.

- Keep a clear focus on the vision.
- Engage only in activities which contribute to the vision.
- There are many good things to invest in, but only a few contribute to the vision.
- Poor stewardship leads us to be driven by opportunities rather than vision.
- Wisely consider the implications of each decision, not merely the easiest path.
- Emotions can easily deceive us, so we must be "clear-minded and self- controlled" (1 Pet. 4:7).
- The path of least resistance often carries a high price to pay.[3]

III. Determine Your Core Values.

A great challenge of all church plant teams is to determine what values will drive their work. While other values may be important, no church can live into every value a team member might hold dear. Your team will need to determine what your collective (cooperate) values are primary to your vision. No

---

2 *Ripe for Harvest*, p. 44.
3 *Ripe for Harvest*, p. 67.

church can do ten things well. Clarity is king in all church planting efforts.

As you determine your values you must avoid comparison. The expression "comparison is the thief of joy," attributed to Theodore Roosevelt, is applicable to many areas of life but is particularly applicable in ministry and more so specifically in the context of church planting.

Your team will need to wrestle through various personal values that are important to individual team members and arrive at your collective values. This is more difficult than it may appear at first glance as everyone on your team has a history which informs their views. Asking good questions through this journey will be helpful and your team exercise time will assist you in the process.

Whether consciously or not, we all approach church planting through our experiences evidenced in statements like, "in my old church we did this or that" or "we used to do things this way or that way" and the like. In all things your team will need to be driven by the collective values of your church plant and avoid comparison.

Seminar 2
Building Your Team[1]
Rev. Luke Raughley

Success often involves working as a team. The saying "Together Everyone Accomplishes More (TEAM)" is more than a convenient acrostic to describe a healthy team dynamic. Much has been written about the need for and the success of effective teamwork. Each of us can point to teams in a variety of contexts, (i.e. sport, business, military, research, education, etc.). Some of these teams operate effectively and create great results, while others struggle and without correction will leave members frustrated and disengaged. The same is true for church planting teams. Teams are not only a good idea experientially, but there are also biblical principles that point to the fact that we are designed and intended to work as a team. Let us look at some scriptures that give principles for effective church plant teams.

I. Clarity

If even lifeless instruments, such as the flute or the harp, do not give distinct notes, how will anyone know what is played? And if the bugle gives an indistinct sound, who will get ready for battle? (1 Cor. 14:7-8).

Paul uses the example of musical instruments playing together to emphasize the need for a clear call. Both a small ensemble and a large orchestra need to play on clear and agreed upon sheet music. If that isn't done disastrous results ensue. Beautiful music can quickly turn into a noisy mess that isn't pleasant for anyone. Without clear orders a strong military force can become confused, not advance, and be

---

1 For more on *Building the Team for Success* see the seminar in *Ripe for Harvest*, pp. 169-180.

defeated. Effective teams have a clear vision of what they are working, learning, or playing toward. Without clarity of purpose and vision, people have a difficult time in any endeavor.

II. Belonging

For the body does not consist of one member but of many. If the foot should say, "Because I am not a hand, I do not belong to the body," that would not make it any less a part of the body. And if the ear should say, "Because I am not an eye, I do not belong to the body," that would not make it any less a part of the body. If the whole body were an eye, where would be the sense of hearing? If the whole body were an ear, where would be the sense of smell? (1 Cor. 12:14-17).

Much can be said of 1 Corinthians 12:11-27 and how it speaks to the nature of teams and the nature of the church. In verses 14-17 Paul speaks to the sense of belonging. In almost ridiculous fashion, the foot and ear claim they aren't part of the body. In the same way, it is ridiculous when parts of the church or parts of your team say, 'I'm not part of the team". Yet all too often that is exactly how some teammates feel. Not knowing how a teammate belongs within the team will lead to disengagement and the potential loss of that teammate.

III. Valuing Diverse Gifts

1 Corinthians 12:11-27, Ephesians 4:11-16, 1 Peter 4:9-11, and Romans 12:3-8 all talk about having different gifts and how important the different gifts are for building up the body. They also address the need for those gifts to be valued and coordinated so that everyone uses their gifts in such a way that the entire team benefits. Likewise, a church plant team needs different gifts and talents. It is important to value those gifts that are different from yours and coordinate those

differences so that everyone is working together for the common goal of building the church.

Team leaders may want to utilize spiritual gift inventories and temperament assessments such as CliftonStrengths (formerly StrengthsFinder) or a Myers-Briggs-like assessment to discover the unique makeup of their team.

IV. Implementing and Adapting

Nehemiah implemented a very aggressive plan to rebuild the walls around Jerusalem (Neh. 4:15-23). Despite the massive undertaking the team was highly motivated and passionately engaged in the task. As Nehemiah and his team, the Israelites, made progress, they also faced opposition.

Nehemiah's team needed to adapt their approach to address the threat of attack. Nehemiah reorganized and coordinated the building crew and the protection detail and created safety and a ready response if needed. Because of the adaptation, the vital work carried on despite the added challenges. Successful teams have a plan, heartily work the plan, and adjust that plan as needed to face the new challenges as they arise.

V. Communication and Coordination

In each of the scriptures shared above there is an implied communication and coordination. We may have a sense of clarity, but that comes because the vision is communicated. There may be a sense of belonging, but that comes through verbal and non-verbal communication that create a sense of closeness and unity. Likewise, in the example of the body, the gifts are intended to be used to build the body operating in a coordinated way. That happens only when there are good lines of communication. Only through well-organized coordination and strong communication was Nehemiah able to accomplish the work and adapt in the face of adversity.

VI. Authorized and Apostolic

Now there were in the church at Antioch prophets and teachers, Barnabas, Simeon who was called Niger, Lucius of Cyrene, Manaen a lifelong friend of Herod the tetrarch, and Saul. While they were worshiping the Lord and fasting, the Holy Spirit said, "Set apart for me Barnabas and Saul for the work to which I have called them." Then after fasting and praying they laid their hands on them and sent them off (Acts 13:1-3).

These are characteristics that are unique to church planting teams. While many teams are focused on a variety of purposes and goals, a church plant team is Christ centered and focused on the work of making disciples of Jesus. Not just anyone engages in this work, but rather those that have been authorized by the larger church and have a heart to be sent out to teach others to obey all that Jesus commanded. Successful church plant teams are led by the Holy Spirit to the work that they engage in.

VII. Evaluation

And after some days Paul said to Barnabas, "Let us return and visit the brothers in every city where we proclaimed the word of the Lord, and see how they are" (Acts 15:36).

Paul clearly shows the need for assessment and evaluation. Every successful team evaluates if they accomplished what they set out to do. If they have, they should celebrate and decide what can be done to build upon that success. If there is more to be done to reach their goals, then they decide the next steps to take to ultimately reach their goal. Likewise, your team will need to determine how you are doing as a team, how you can improve, and how you can be even more effective in the next endeavor.

Throughout Scripture we see examples where the Lord joins people together with others. Moses had Aaron, David had Jonathan, Elijah had Elisha, Paul had Barnabas, Silas and others. Even our Lord and Savior Jesus called together his twelve disciples. Together they had a much greater impact than they would have on their own. As a church plant team seeks to proclaim the good news about Jesus, our witness is practically demonstrated to the world by our love for one another. To establish a community of believers you must first model what it means to be a community of believers. This can be a fluid group with new teammates being added and others moving on. The key is to work with the team that the Lord has given you now and begin there like Paul did in his various journeys.[2]

"The church plant team must believe that God knew what he was doing when he established team as a primary ministry principle. Being together as teams is more than just a good idea, it's God's ideal. As such, when hard times come, team leaders will fight for the unity of their team, affirm, and love their team. For in their hearts, they believe that God has ordained it."[3]

---

[2] See "Paul's Team Members: Companions, Laborers, and Fellow Workers" in *The Timothy Conference Workbook*, p. 129.

[3] *The Timothy Conference Workbook*, p. 65.

Seminar 3
Building Resilience
Rev. Jordan King

Resilience is not an innate quality or gift that pastors and leaders are born with. Instead, resilience is built through experience, hurt, and reliance on God and others to meet our spiritual and emotional needs. Every leader needs to develop the ability to withstand and recover from the challenges that come with ministry. Developing healthy patterns for your ministry and family is key to building resilience and preventing burnout as "Fatigue makes cowards of us all."[1]

I. Biblical Patterns of Resilient Leaders

   A. Moses became exhausted from overwork and had to learn to delegate leadership and lean on the support of trusted people in his life. He had an intimate relationship with God that refreshed him despite the challenges of leading a stubborn and difficult people (Exod. 18:13-23; 17:8-13).

   B. David was unjustly hunted for years by King Saul but despite the opposition continued to trust God. When his own son attempted to kill him, he relied on his friends and entrusted his life to God. When he sinned against God he repented and turned back to God for healing (Ps. 18:1-6; 51:7-12; 2 Sam. 15:18-23).

   C. Jesus consistently retreated from the crowds to rest and pray. We see examples of him fasting, praying, and retreating. When his crucifixion was close, He spent time in prayer and asked His disciples to help share His burden. He exemplified the need to be connected to God

---
1 This quote is attributed to Vince Lombardi.

to bear fruit (Matt. 14:13; Luke 22:39-46; Matt. 4:1; John 15:1-4).

D. Paul never did ministry in isolation from others, and always had co-laborers in ministry work. He endured suffering consistently, relying on God and others for support in seasons of suffering. He deeply understood the need to depend on the grace and working of the Spirit to accomplish the work of ministry (2 Cor. 1:8-11; Acts 16:1-5).

II. Developing Patterns That Promote Resiliency

A. Rely on the Holy Spirit for heart and community change. Plant the seeds but trust God to bring the growth. We serve faithfully but entrust the fruit of our work to God (1 Cor. 3:5-9; 1 Cor. 2:1-5).

B. Delegate and then delegate again. Train and authorize others to lead so that you can focus on teaching and shepherding work, and so that others can share the burdens of leadership (Acts 6:1-4, Eph 4:11-13).

C. Find someone who is ahead of you in life and ministry and allow them to disciple and shepherd you as you serve. Every leader needs to be mentored and pastored by someone (Matt.10; Titus 2:1-8; 2 Tim. 1:1-8). If you need help finding a mentor or shepherd who understands the challenges you will face in church planting and can walk with you, your Evangel Field Coach may be able to assist you with finding someone who may be a good fit for your specific needs and context.

D. Shepherd your family as your first ministry priority. Do not give your families the crumbs that are left over and do not treat them as obstacles to your ministry. Be present and available to enjoy your family life and invest in their lives (1 Tim. 3:2-5, 12; Prov. 3:1-8; Eph. 6:4; Col. 3:18-21).

E. Build in seasonal rhythms of rest and a Sabbath pattern. Spend intentional time to rest, pray, and then reengage in the work of ministry. In retreat from our work, we trust God, and reorient our hearts and minds towards Him (Gen. 2:1-3; Eccles. 3:1-8; Heb. 4:6-10; Mark 6:40-47).

F. Stay connected to the vine so that you will bear fruit. If we neglect time in prayer and the word, we will begin to minister out of an empty cup. We should minister to others out of the overflow God has accomplished in our own hearts (Ps. 1:1-4; John 15:1-5).

III. Healing from Relational Hurts and Losses

A. Grieve well and take the time to process your pain with God and others. There is a temptation in ministry to simply move onto the next busy season. Make sure you give room to process and grieve difficult circumstances and experiences (2 Cor. 7:6-7; Isa. 38:14; Rom. 12:15).

B. Avoid isolation and surround yourself with trusted people who care deeply for your well-being. Isolation is our normal response to hurt, but it will lead to unhealthy habits and ministry patterns. Living in isolation breeds the lie that we are alone in our pain and no one else understands (1 Kings 19:9-18; 2 Cor. 1:3-11).

C. Understand your calling and embrace the reality that suffering is normal. A sense of calling and purpose allows us to embrace the realities that ministry will be difficult. A sense of calling allows us to see beyond the moment and continue to run our race well (2 Thess. 1:11; Heb. 12:1-3).

PLANT

TEAM EXERCISES: PREPARE

Team Exercise 1
Establishing Context

Team Exercise 2
Defining Values and Vision

Team Exercise 3
Team Effectiveness

Team Exercise 4
Building Resilience

Exercise 1
Establishing Context[1]

Your team will need to understand its context, the target community, and the challenges the selected context might present.

Instructions

Discuss the following questions and document your answers. Be specific.

1. What are your target communities?
2. What do you know about those communities (demographic information)?
3. What do you need to learn about those communities?
4. What ethnic or people group(s) will you target, and why?
5. What will distinguish you from other churches?
6. What will your expression[2] of the church look like?
7. With what network, denomination, or association will your church be affiliated?

Other Charting Your Course Questions

a. Do you have church bylaws, and statement of faith in place? If not, how will you develop them internally?

---

1 Adapted from an Evangel School exercise in *Ripe for Harvest*, pp. 79–92.
2 For a discussion of the various church expressions see *Ripe for Harvest*, pp. 87–92.

b. When will you incorporate[3] and apply for tax exempt status via a determination letter?

c. How will you oversee the proper handling of finances[4] and church accounts?

d. Will you pursue a 501c3 status?

Develop and document your goals for the next 6-12 months based on your discussions. Make sure your goals are measurable, include specific due dates, and indicate the people who will be responsible for the goal. It is okay to postpone a decision until after the Evangel School as long as you establish a goal and date by which a decision needs to be made.

---

3   See "Church and State" in *Planting Churches among the City's Poor: An Anthology of Urban Church Planting Resources, Vol. 2*, Wichita: TUMI Press, 2015, p. 358.

4   See "Church Financial Process" in *Planting Churches among the City's Poor, Vol. 2*, p. 351.

Exercise 2
***Defining Values and Vision*[1]**

Your team will need to clearly articulate the values and vision that guide your church.

Instructions

Complete the Team Exercise: Defining Values/Vision.

1. Each team member should select and rank 7 values from the list below.

2. As a team discuss everyone's list to brainstorm and determine the team's core values.

   a. Which values does your team have in common?

   b. Are there values important to your team in addition to those listed?

   c. Create a list of 5 core values that will guide your church plant.

3. Develop your church vision statement based on your core values.

   a. Where do you see the church in 5 years?

   b. What would "success" look like?

   c. What differences should there be in your internal and external language?

---

1 Adapted from an Evangel School exercise in *Ripe for Harvest*, pp. 95-102.

Seeing the Big Picture: Defining Values/Vision Chart

Rank order the following from 1-7 ("1" – most important). Only choose seven, even though they are all important. Avoid combining values!

___ Teaching God's Word
___ Fellowship
___ Cell church or small groups
___ Worship
___ Prayer
___ Training/equipping members to use gifts
___ Ministry to young people and children
___ Stable leadership
___ Reputation in the community
___ Use of spiritual gifts
___ Multi-cultural representation
___ Worship style
___ Preaching style
___ Worship format
___ Charismatic orientation
___ Ethnic/cultural focus
___ Group structures
___ Evangelistic strategy
___ Justice issues
___ Leadership styles
___ Church government
___ Financial priorities
___ Assimilation and follow-up
___ Spiritual disciplines (study, prayer)
___ Building the body
___ Outreach
___ Ministry to adults
___ Counseling/pastoral care
___ Music ministry
___ Social justice ministry
___ Discipleship
___ Administration
___ World missions
___ Reaching out to the community
___ Planning and setting goals
___ Assimilating new attendees
___ Close relationships
___ Doctrinal purity
___ Varied programs
___ Other(s):

Develop and document your goals for the next 6-12 months based on your discussions. Make sure your goals are measurable, include specific due dates, and indicate the people who will be responsible for the goal. It is okay to postpone a decision until after the Evangel School as long as you establish a goal and date by which a decision needs to be made.

Exercise 3
Team Effectiveness[1]

Your team will need an objective method to evaluate itself to determine who needs to be added to your church plant team and the roles they will play.

1. SWOT Analysis

Discuss areas of internal strengths and weakness (things you can control, like resources, calling, gifting, etc.) and external strengths and weakness (things you cannot control like the economy, local ordinances, openness of the area to the gospel, etc.)

    a. Internal Strengths (things you can control)

    b. Internal Weaknesses (things you can control)

    c. External Opportunities (things outside your control)

    d. External Threats (things outside your control)

    e. What were 2 or 3 of the most important things you learned about your team?

2. Building the Team Discussion Questions

    a. What are the various roles and responsibilities of our current team members?

    b. What roles or skills do you lack, and how will you fill those positions or roles?

    c. Are team members operating in roles aligned with their gifting?

---

1 Adapted from an Evangel School exercise in *Ripe for Harvest*, pp. 188-205.

d. How will you continue to assess the effectiveness of your team as you move forward? What tools will you use to do so?

e. Discuss who potential teammates might be for various needed roles in your church.

f. What is your church governance model?

g. Describe how your team makes decisions.

h. When, where, and how often will your team meet for training and encouragement?

i. What kind of training or preparation tools does your team need to strengthen and develop our team?

j. In what areas does your team need to grow?

k. How will you evaluate your success as a team?

Develop and document your goals for the next 6-12 months based on your discussions. Make sure your goals are measurable, include specific due dates, and indicate the people who will be responsible for the goal. It is okay to postpone a decision until after the Evangel School as long as you establish a goal and date by which a decision needs to be made.

Exercise 4
Building Resilience

Your team will need to establish healthy patterns of ministry as you work together to plant and lead your church. It is vital that your team is aware and as prepared as they can be for the physical, emotional, and spiritual demands of church planting and how you can maintain healthy patterns together.

Instructions

Take time to discuss the questions below as a team toward developing an action plan to establish healthy patterns of ministry.

1. What spiritual rhythms do you need to prioritize developing within your team (Sabbath, Retreat, Prayer, Fasting, Time in the Word)?

2. How can your team support and encourage the development of healthy family rhythms?

3. What people are in place to support and encourage your team in developing healthy spiritual and family rhythms? If your team does not have them, how will you grow your support system?

4. Are there any trainings or tools that would be helpful for your team?

5. Based on the seminar on resilience are there any patterns or things we are doing that need to change?

Develop and document your goals for the next 6-12 months based on your discussions. Make sure your goals are measurable, include specific due dates, and indicate the people who will be responsible for the goal. It is okay to postpone a decision until after the Evangel School as long as you establish a goal and date by which a decision needs to be made.

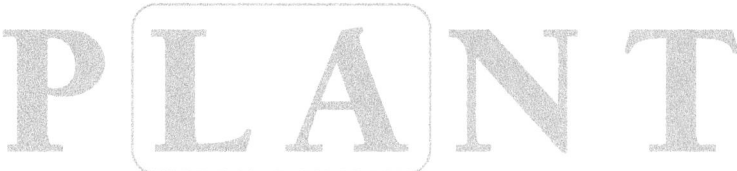

SESSION 2: LAUNCH AND ASSEMBLE

In this session, we will give our attention to the driving force of the gospel, navigating culture and context, and developing a strategy for evangelism and follow-up.

Seminar 4
The Driving Force of the Gospel

Seminar 5
Navigating Culture and Context

Seminar 6
Evangelism and Follow-up

Seminar 4
The Driving Force of the Gospel
Pastor Lorenzo Elizondo

The gospel is all about Jesus. The gospel is the central theme of Scripture because all the Bible points to Jesus. The gospel is the good news that our great God looked at fallen humanity with compassion, sent his Son Jesus to live the life we could not live, and to pay the price we could not pay, and victoriously rise again, defeating Satan, sin, and death, and overcoming the cosmic separation between God and humanity. This is the good news that saves us.

The gospel not only saves us, but also sends us to fulfill the mission of Christ. Unfortunately, many Christians today view the gospel as merely a presentation tool for conversion. But it is so much more than the ABCs of Christianity, it is the A to the Z of the Christian faith. As the Apostle Paul reminds us in Romans 1:16, "For I am not ashamed of the gospel, for it is the very power of God for salvation to everyone who believes, to the Jew first and also to the Greek."

The gospel not only saves us and sends us, but it also shapes us as the church. In other words, the Church exists through the gospel, and for the gospel. The church is like a heart. If a heart only brought blood to itself, the body would die. And, if the heart only pumped blood out, the body would likewise die. A heart must pump blood in and out for the body to remain alive. Similarly, the church must constantly come to the gospel for life, and then be sent out with it to remain alive. Like the heart, Jesus made us to live in a rhythm. He told us to love God, our neighbor, and one another (the church).

From the book of Acts to today, the story of the church is a story of a people who gave their lives to the proclamation, preservation, and propagation of the gospel. Churches and church planters are driven by many things. Some are driven by a vision of a better tomorrow, better neighborhoods, or even better churches. All of these are good things, but ultimately what must drive us must be the gospel. Therefore, it is essential that we understand the message, the mission, and the means of the gospel. For it is the gospel that teaches us what to believe, how to see the world around us, and what the church should be.

I. The Message of the Gospel

A. The Bible contains one single unfolding drama, the story of God. From Genesis to Revelation, the will of God to redeem humanity is evident.

B. Jesus is the ultimate champion of the story of God.

C. Our Lord made it clear that the entire biblical story is about Him.

D. It has been said that if the New Testament is Jesus Christ *revealed*, the Old Testament is Jesus Christ *concealed*.[1] From beginning to end, our Bible is an epic story about Jesus.

E. And why is Jesus so central, so ultimate, so unequaled in the biblical story and in hearts around the world? Because only he came to earth, truly God and truly man, and lived a perfect life; died an atoning death; and rose to vanquish sin, Satan, darkness, and death. Jesus was everything Adam failed to be, everything Israel failed to be, and everything we have failed to be. He succeeded where we have not. The Author who designed us to worship and enjoy him—and

---

1 Augustine's statement from "Questions on the Heptateuch," 2.73 in *The Works of St. Augustine: Writings On The Old Testament*.

whom we have offended because of our rebellion—stepped into his own story to salvage it.

II. The Mission of the Gospel

A. The Gospel is the good news that saves us and sends us to fulfill the mission of Christ.

Jesus summarized his mission by stating, "He came to seek and to save the lost." (Luke 19:10).

B. For the proclamation of the Gospel to be heard and understood, the gospel must be contextualized.

When considering the process of contextualization, many people rightly think of the Apostle Paul. After all it was Paul who said, "To the weak I become weak that I might win the weak. I have become all things to all people, that by all means I might save some. I do it all for the sake of the gospel, that I may share with them in its blessings" (1 Cor. 9:19-23). But it was also Paul who said, "Be imitators of me as I imitate Christ" (1 Cor. 11:1). In other words, Jesus was Paul's perfect model of contextualization.

John writes, "And the Word became flesh and dwelt among us, and we have seen his glory, glory as of the only Son from the Father, full of grace and truth" (John 1:14). Through the incarnation of Christ, we see the kingdom of heaven entering the world. In Christ we see the light of the world is stepping into our brokenness and sin to bring redemption and freedom. Jesus came near us, breaking the barriers that separated sinful people from a holy God.

C. Jesus said, "As the Father has sent me, so I am sending you" (John 20:21).

Jesus is sending us into our cities and neighborhoods to take the message of the gospel. But in order for us to effectively carry out the mission of Christ, we must become wise in our understanding the cultural landscape. Contextualization not only requires an exegesis[2] of the Scriptures to better understand the gospel, but also an exegesis of our culture to better understand the people we are trying to reach. This exegetical process will help us to see our culture through the missionary lenses of the gospel.

III. The Means of the Gospel

A. The gospel not only saves us and sends us, but it also shapes us. Jesus calls us to the gospel (loving Jesus), to the culture (loving our neighbor), and to the church (loving our brothers and sisters).

When we are saved, and before we are sent, we are shaped by the gospel within the context of the local church. The church is God's primary plan for reaching the World. Jesus said, "I will build my church and the gates of hell shall not prevail against it" (Matt. 16:18).

B. Gospel and Mission do not flow out of a vacuum. They are the focus and purpose of the church, the fuel and fire of God's people who have been joined to Christ and his Church.

---

2 Exegesis is a critical explanation or interpretation of a biblical text in which one seeks to understand the meaning of a passage in its own setting to draw out key principles. For more information on the exegetical process, see Rev. Dr. Don L. Davis, *Bible Interpretation*. The Capstone Curriculum, Module 5. (Wichita: TUMI Press, 2005).

The church is a vital part of Christian mission because it reveals the nature of the inbreaking rule of God. Mission takes place as people see our love for God, our neighbor, and one another. Therefore, it is vital for the church to be aware that the gospel is communicated both through the words that we say and the lives that we live. In this manner, the invisible God is made visible through the love of the people of God (1 John 4:12).

C. The church is more than a gathering place, it is the visible expression of the kingdom of God in the neighborhood.

Like an embassy embodying and representing the interests of their sovereign country on foreign land, the church is God's embassy on the block. The church is God's ambassadors, representing His Kingdom in real time, with real people, as we live out the power and implications of the gospel in this world.

"The Church is the Community of the Kingdom but never the Kingdom itself. The Kingdom is God's reign and the realm in which the blessings of his reign are experienced; the church is the fellowship of those who have experienced God's rule and reign and entered the enjoyment of its blessings. The Kingdom creates the church, works through the church, and is proclaimed in the world by the church."[3]

IV. Conclusion

The driving force of the gospel is present in the Scriptures, because as Jesus said, "they testify about me" (John 5:39). From Genesis to Revelation the Scriptures point to Jesus, our Savior and King. So, as you preach, teach, and make disciples,

---

[3] *Mere Missions*, p. 148.

have the mindset of the Apostle Paul who said, "For I decided to know nothing among you except Jesus and him crucified" (1 Cor. 2:2).

The driving force of the gospel is present in the mission of the church as we follow the example of Jesus who came to seek and to save that which was lost. The gospel saves us and sends us. Jesus rescues us from sin and commissions us to make disciples of all the nations. The mission of the church is not just to gather and grow a group of people, rather we are to fulfill the mission of Jesus as we take the unchanging truths of the gospel in understandable ways to the ever-changing cultural contexts we have been called to.

Finally, the driving force of the gospel is present in the church as we demonstrate our love for God, for our neighbor, and for one another.

Seminar 5
Navigating Culture and Context[1]
Pastor Lorenzo Elizondo

We live in a diverse and ever-changing world. The human landscape of our global cities has dramatically changed in recent years. The majority of the world's population has chosen to live in large global cities, creating a more urbanized world. This shift and growth in population has not only produced a vast diversity of people, ethnicities, and backgrounds but also a vast diversity of culture as well. While "diversity" has become a buzzword in our modern times, and while most people believe that understanding the diversity of people and cultures is important, few can define culture or explain what it is. In order for the church to effectively demonstrate and declare the gospel to the people(s) and place(s) God has called them to reach, we must become skilled navigators of culture.

I. What Is Culture?

A. Dr. Davis defines culture: "Culture is that integrated, well-established, and communally defined patterns of behavior and worldview which influences the cognitive, affective, and evaluative dimensions of its expression." Simply stated, culture is the learned patterns and behaviors that shape our values and worldview, which form the way of life for a society.

B. Where do these learned patterns and behaviors come from, and how are they developed? Dr. Davis explains that there are three dimensions of culture.

---

[1] This seminar is rooted in the concepts of the seminar "The Difference That Difference Makes" in *Ripe for Harvest*, pp. 139-153.

1. The Cognitive Dimension is what a culture knows and considers to be real and true. The cognitive dimension is shaped by:

2. The Affective Dimension is the emotions and expression of feelings about what a culture finds beauty in and what it dislikes as well.

3. The Evaluative Dimension – The values by which a culture judges human relationships to be moral and immoral (evaluation of right and wrong).

C. Ultimately, culture is about values. To understand culture, we have to understand what matters to people and why they place value in those things. Whatever it is that matters most to a group of people, that which they love, esteem, defend, live, and die for, will by definition, define and create its culture.

II. Understanding Cultural Differences

To effectively navigate culture, not only must we understand what culture is, we must also understand the differences in culture.

A. Differences are good because God created us with differences, Acts 17.

B. The differences between cultures (people) are real and significant.

C. Minimizing or ignoring our cultural differences can have harmful effects on the gospel.

III. Establishing a Distinctly Christian Culture

But for the Christian, for those who love and value Jesus Christ above all else, culture is not defined by human achievement. Rather it is defined by three simple words, Jesus is Lord. The church has its unique reason for being, and it is found in those three simple words that make up the ontological reality that defines, develops, and drives a distinctly Christian culture.

A. First and foremost, Christian culture is distinctly different from the world because it is supernatural in nature.

B. Second, the reality that Jesus is Lord not only defines the church, it also develops the church. The church has a distinctly Christian culture because it does not exist for itself since it was not created by itself.

C. Lastly, the reality that Jesus is Lord drives the church. The church – God's redeemed people – transcends every political, ethnic, socioeconomic, and gender-cultural construct. Not because it's better or superior in and of itself, but because of its distinct submission to the authority and sufficiency of the Scriptures.

IV. Conclusion

The goal of cultural navigation is to understand that every context has a culture and that to have an effective witness of the gospel we must be aware that cultural differences exist so that we can fulfill our ultimate goal, which is to bring people to Christlikeness, not cultural sameness. Our aim is not for people to lose their cultural distinctives, but rather for them to submit to Jesus as Lord. Just as Jesus came to us, overcoming our cultural barriers, so we must overcome the cultural barriers of our day to effectively demonstrate and declare the gospel. By prioritizing the authority of Scripture and pursuing Christlikeness, believers can overcome cultural barriers to demonstrate and declare the gospel effectively.

Seminar 6
Evangelism and Follow-Up[1]

As discussed in previous seminars, in the Prepare stage of church planting you will need to develop a team of faithful Christians to help you pursue the vision of planting a church. As we move into the Launch and Assemble phases of the church plant, however, you should avoid the temptation to grow the church by recruiting believers from other churches and relational networks to join your church. While there is nothing wrong with welcoming Christians who are seeking a healthy church to belong to and serve, you should not confuse doing so with true church growth. Churches exist to help the lost (non-believers) come to saving faith in the Lord Jesus. Therefore, evangelism and incorporating new believers into the family of God should be the measure of growth and effectiveness.

As many Christians wrestle with much fear related to evangelism, helping your team and church members understand the nature of evangelism and how to share their faith are paramount in church planting. Each context will offer its own set of unique challenges to those sharing the gospel. The following outline is offered to both remove the stigma associated with evangelism and prepare you to create a strategy for incorporating new believers into your church.

I. Evangelism – The *Oikos* factor

    A. The *Oikos* factor: the central distinguishing social feature in dynamic evangelical witness

---

1 Adapted from a seminar by Rev. Dr. Don L. Davis in *Ripe for Harvest*, pp. 242-247.

> A household usually contained four generations, including men, married women, unmarried daughters, slaves of both sexes, persons without citizenship, and 'sojourners,' or resident foreign workers.
>
> ~ Hans Walter Wolff. Anthology of the Old Testament.

The gospel in our NT narratives is described as coming through and to the various people in the household where they resided, (cf. Mark 5:19; Luke 19:9; John 4:53; John 1;41-45, etc.). Cornelius' example is a prime case, Acts 10-11.

1. The dimensions of our natural, human relational webs

    a. *Common kinship relationships* (immediate, extended, and adopted families)

    b. *Common friendships* (friends, neighbors, special interests)

    c. *Common associates* (work relationships, special interests, recreation, ethnic or cultural alliances, national allegiances)

2. Why *oikos* (household) evangelism via relational webs is effective

    a. *Oikos* evangelism is biblical – Jesus and apostles ministered in this fashion.

    b. *Oikos* is our most natural and least threatening network of existing relationships (no cold calling, or the truest form of lifestyle and friendship evangelism).

c. *Oikos* individuals are usually receptive to other members (builds on shared history, experience, and concerns).

d. *Oikos* relationships are "built in" or resident mission field.

e. *Oikos* relationships make follow-up less strained, impersonal.

f. *Oikos* allows entire family groups to be targeted.

g. *Oikos* relationships constantly re-seed new contact base.

Reminiscence: How did the gospel come to you? Trace your own *oikos* linkages!

---

3. Implications for urban *evangelism*

   a. Think "economically" in every personal relationship you make and cultivate; seek to win the *oikos*, not just the individual.

   b. Lay proper foundation for continued influence within the relational web.

   c. Aim for the entire *oikos*, even while seeking solid individual conversions.

   d. Encourage every convert to become an Andrew (John 1:40-43) to their own *oikos*.

   e. Expect God, the Holy Spirit, to move the message of the good news naturally through the *oikos* relationships of the converts you see.

II. Follow-Up: Incorporating and Nurturing in the Family of God

A. Definition: *Incorporation into the family of God for the purpose of edification and fruitfulness, to the glory of God*

1. *Incorporation into the family of God* – introduction and welcome into the family of God, Rom. 15:5-7

   a. Making visible what has in fact become actual

   b. Welcome as central factor of koinonia (fellowship), 1 John 1:1-4

2. For the purpose of *edification and fruitfulness*

   a. Edification – to build up another to the fullness of Christ, to maturity in Christ (Christlikeness), Eph. 4:9-15

   b. Fruitfulness – to be used of God to raise up as many disciples as possible as quickly as we can for the sake of fulfilling the Great Commission, John 15:16

3. *To the glory of God* – the end of all things, Rom. 11:36

B. Why Follow-up is necessary

1. Need for protection: new converts are vulnerable to attack (e.g., the parable of the soils, Matt. 13)

   a. The devil's lies and schemes

   b. The cares of the world

   c. The lack of depth and substance

   d. The proneness towards error

2. Need to reorient their lives around their new identity in Christ: new converts require a sense of belonging and security, 2 Cor. 6:14-18

3. Need for ongoing instruction, nurture, and feeding: new converts need to understand God's word and will, 1 Pet. 2:2; Heb. 5:11-6:4

4. Need for friends and cultivating new life patterns based on a kingdom perspective: new converts need friends to encourage holy living, John 13:34-35

5. Need for regular, parental and pastoral care: new converts need godly pastors to keep watch over their souls, Heb. 13:17

C. Dynamics of Follow-up

1. Attachment to a local assembly of believers, Heb. 10:24-25

2. Immediate, consistent contact after decision

3. Doctrinal nurture and teaching

4. Strategic befriending

5. *Oikos* recognition and penetration

6. Feeding and care

7. Establishing new relationships in the Body of Christ

D. The Follow-up operations

1. Baptism

2. Deeper understanding in the doctrine of salvation and the Kingdom

3. Befriending in the body: forming new relationships with the believers

    a. Cell group

    b. Personal relationships

    c. Body life

    d. Membership

4. The Eucharist (Communion) and the discipline of worship in the Body of Christ

5. Sharing one's personal faith

6. Instruction in the disciplines of the spiritual life

7. Connection with pastoral care: edification and oversight

E. Principles and practices of Follow-up

1. Understand the goal of discipleship: Disciples, not converts, Matt. 28:18-20

2. Learn the basics yourself: make certain you are followed up, Luke 6:40

3. Focus on the Word of God, not methods and strategies, 1 Pet. 2:2

4. Treat every convert as a newborn in Christ: abandon none

5. Raise your own spiritual children, or find surrogate parents to raise them

6. Recognize the effectiveness of following up in a cell group

    a. Friendships

    b. Camaraderie

    c. Shared experience

    d. Maximize curricula, time, and resources

    e. Development of leadership

7. Focus on the *oikos* even in follow-up activities

PLANT

TEAM EXERCISES: LAUNCH AND ASSEMBLE

Team Exercise 5
The Driving Force of the Gospel

Team Exercise 6
Navigating Culture and Context

Team Exercise 7
Evangelism and Follow-up

Exercise 5
The Driving Force of the Gospel

Your team will need to understand the centrality of the gospel and develop a strategy to proclaim the gospel, contextualize it, and live it out as the church functioning as God's embassy in the community.

Instructions

Discuss the following questions as a team and document your answers.

Exercise Questions

1. How does the gospel save and transform our lives?

2. What specific areas of your life and in the church have you seen the transforming power of the gospel?

3. Why is it important to understand that the gospel and the Scriptures are all about Jesus?

4. In what ways have you understood this and seen the importance of it in your life, church, and approach to ministry?

5. What does it mean for the gospel to send you and what is your mission?

6. How can you actively participate in fulfilling this mission in your own community?

7. Why is the church referred to as God's embassy on earth and how will your church proclaim and demonstrate the gospel?

8. What is contextualization and why is it important when sharing the gospel?

9. How can you better understand and relate to the cultural context of the people with whom you are sharing the gospel?

10. How will you develop a strong sense of gospel identity and mission in your church?

Develop and document your goals for the next 6-12 months based on your discussions. Make sure your goals are measurable, include specific due dates, and indicate the people who will be responsible for the goal. It is okay to postpone a decision until after the Evangel School as long as you establish a goal and date by which a decision needs to be made.

Exercise 6
Navigating Culture and Context

Your team will need to develop a strategy and plan to navigate the culture and context of your selected community.

Discussion Questions

1. Why is it important for Christians to understand and engage with different cultures?

2. What will you do as a church to better understand and appreciate the cultural differences of those around you?

3. What are the specific ways you can contextualize the gospel where you are planting so the community can better understand the gospel in their own language and ways?

4. What are some cultural barriers you may have to overcome in order for you to effectively demonstrate and declare the gospel in your context?

5. How will the reality that Jesus is Lord guide and influence your church?

6. In what ways will this reality define, drive, and develop your church?

7. What can you learn from Jesus's example in overcoming cultural barriers to reach others?

8. How far are you willing to go as a church to share the love of Jesus with others?

Other Assemble Discussion Questions

a. When will you need to have a meeting space?

b. What will you need financially and what equipment do you need to start with initially?

c. What will a typical weekly service look like culturally, and who will be responsible for each element of the service?

Develop and document your goals for the next 6-12 months based on your discussions. Make sure your goals are measurable, include specific due dates, and indicate the people who will be responsible for the goal. It is okay to postpone a decision until after the Evangel School as long as you establish a goal and date by which a decision needs to be made.

Exercise 7
Evangelism and Follow-up[1]

Your team will need to develop a strategy and plan for conducting evangelistic events and follow-up among the target population.

Instructions

Discuss the following questions as a team and document your answers.

1. What evangelistic events will you conduct to add to the church?

2. How will you follow up with new believers?

3. What statistical tools will you use for follow-up?

4. How will you form cell groups or Bible studies to follow up with new believers and to continue evangelism?

5. With whom in the community will you pursue your first evangelistic contacts, and how will you reach them?

6. Are there local, city, state, or church resources that you can use to better serve and reach your neighborhood?

7. How will you follow up with new converts and attendees? Who will be responsible for follow up, and what tools do they need?

8. How will you smoothly incorporate and involve new attendees into the life of the church?

---

1   Adapted from the exercises "Expand the Church" and "Establish the Church" in *Ripe for Harvest*, pp. 288-291 and 296-300.

9. What does it mean to be a church member and what does an attendee need to do to become a member?

Develop and document your goals for the next 6-12 months based on your discussions. Make sure your goals are measurable, include specific due dates, and indicate the people who will be responsible for the goal. It is okay to postpone a decision until after the Evangel School as long as you establish a goal and date by which a decision needs to be made.

PLANT

Session 3: Nurture and Transition (Multiplication)

In this session, we will explore principles related to effective discipling in the church, leadership development, and creating pathways for multiplication.

Seminar 7
Effective Discipling

Seminar 8
Leadership Development

Seminar 9
Creating Pathways for Multiplication

Seminar 7
Effective Discipling[1]

While evangelism and incorporating new believers into the family of God are good measures of initial growth and effectiveness, numerical growth can be deceptive in terms of calculating spiritual growth. Many church planters become consumed with the numbers game and can quickly fall into guilt and shame when blinded my numeric comparisons with other churches. Church planters should always keep in mind that numeric growth is not necessarily an indicator of discipleship. This is a lesson many church planters have learned the hard way.

As difficult as it may be to read, evangelism is not the end of the work of the church. It is merely the beginning. The truest work of the church in responding to the Great Commission of our Lord is to make disciples. Therefore, you will need a strategy for making disciples within the church. The following outline is offered to help your team—and the church as you equip them later—to understand the heart and rhythms of discipleship.

I. **The Great Commission, the Kingdom of God, and the Church of Jesus Christ**

   A. The Great Commission, Matt. 28:18-20; Mark 16:15-16; Luke 24:46-49; Acts 1:8; John 20:21

      1. The authority of Jesus Christ

      2. The mandate to go into all nations, make disciples, and baptize in the name of the Father, Son, and Holy Spirit

---

1 Adapted from a seminar by Rev. Dr. Don L. Davis in *Ripe for Harvest*, pp. 359-367.

3. The directive: to teach to obey everything Christ taught

B. The Kingdom of God, Matt. 6:33; Mark 1:14-15; Rev. 11:15; Rom. 14:17

   1. The Kingdom of God = the reign and rule of God in the midst of his universe

   2. The kingdom of darkness = the reign and rule of our mortal enemy: Satan, the Adversary, the devil and his agents: the rulers of this darkness, Eph. 6:12

C. The Church of Jesus Christ = the Body of Christ: the visible manifestation of the living Christ in the world today, the revelation of God's wisdom in the world, and the agent of God to proclaim reconciliation throughout the earth, Matt. 16:18; Eph. 1:22-23; 1 Tim. 3:15; Eph. 3.8-12; 2 Cor. 5:18-21

Discipleship is the fulfillment of God's plan to restore His reign throughout the earth, by multiplying disciples of Jesus through the church to every nation (people group) on the face of the earth! To make disciples is to fulfill the mandate of the risen Lord till He comes!

II. The Whys and the Whats of Discipling in the Church

A. Why disciple in the church?

   1. The church is the *locus of God's concern in the world* – his desire is to form a new humanity in the church.

   2. The church is the *agent of God in his mission to reconcile the world* to himself.

3. The church is *the body of Christ*, the revelation of himself to a fallen generation.

4. Discipling occurs *in* the church, *through* the church, and *for* the church.

B. What are some biblical examples of discipling?

1. Moses and Joshua, Num. 27:15-20; cf. Josh. 1:1-2

2. Elijah and Elisha, 1 Kings 19; 2 Kings 2

3. David and his "mighty men", 1 Chron. 12

4. Naomi and Ruth, Ruth 1

5. Jesus and the Twelve, Mark 3:14

6. Paul and Timothy (and his band), Acts 20:4; cf. Phil. 2:20-22

Discipling in the church is the process of modeling, mentoring, and befriending another in the church in order to enable them to become incorporated into the Body of Christ, to become established in the faith, and then to be equipped to minister in Christ's name in the church and world, as the Holy Spirit will lead.

III. The Role of the Discipler: Model, Mentor, and Friend

A. The responsibility to be a *Model* (who the discipler is)

B. The responsibility to be a *Mentor* (what the discipler does)

C. The responsibility to be a *Friend* (how the discipler relates)

IV. The Role of the Local Church in Effective Discipling

A. The Church helps incorporate new converts into the body.

B. The Church is pivotal in establishing new Christians in the faith: "proving the authenticity in the faith."

C. The Church equips the saints to minister, Eph. 4:9-15

Christlikeness:
The Ultimate Aim of All Discipling in the Church

The Christian is united to Christ by virtue of their faith in Him. Only when we understand that God's overarching desire is to conform every member of His church to the beauty and glory of Christ can we place discipleship in its proper context. The Christian is united to Christ in all dimensions of His life and ministry, and so discipleship is effectively seeking to make visible in our lives what God has done in our position in Christ (Rom. 8:29; 1 John 3:2-3; 2 Cor. 3:18; Phil. 3:4-12).

Seminar 8
Leadership Development[1]

Discipleship occurs at many levels within the church. Beyond the practice of making disciples within the church as discussed in the previous seminar, every church will need a leadership development strategy. Creating a leadership pipeline and a process to identify, equip, and on-board those gifted for leadership in your church is essential to longevity and next-generation leadership. The following outline is offered to help you move toward creating a strategy to identify, equip, and commission leaders for the work God calls them to do.

Developing Leaders in Urban Church Plants: From Commission to Community

I. **Commission**

    A. Definition: Recognized the call of God and replies with prompt obedience to his lordship and leading.

    B. Key Scriptures to keep in mind: 2 Tim. 1:6-14; 1 Tim. 4:14; Acts 1:8; Matt. 28:18-20

    C. Critical concept: on the authority of God – God's leader acts on God's recognized call and authority, acknowledged by the saints and God's leaders.

    D. Central elements:

        1. A clear call from God

        2. Authentic testimony before God and others

---

1 Adapted from a seminar by Rev. Dr. Don L. Davis in *Ripe for Harvest*, pp. 377-381.

3. Deep sense of personal conviction based on Scripture

4. Personal burden for a particular task or people

5. Confirmation by leaders and the body

E. Satanic strategy to abort: Operate on the basis of personality or position rather than on God's appointed call and ongoing authority

F. Key steps:

1. Identify God's call.

2. Discover your burden.

3. Be confirmed by leadership.

G. Results: deep confidence towards God arising from God's call

II. Character

A. Definition: reflects the character of Christ in their personal convictions, conduct, and lifestyle

B. Key Scriptures to keep in mind: John 15:4-5; 2 Tim. 2:2; 1 Cor. 4:2; Gal. 5:16-23

C. Critical concept: In the humility of Christ – God's leader demonstrates the mind and lifestyle of Christ in his or her actions and relationships.

D. Central elements:

1. Passion for Christlikeness

2. Radical lifestyle for the Kingdom

3. Serious pursuit of holiness

4. Discipline in the personal life

5. Fulfills role-relationships as bond-slave of Jesus Christ

6. Provides an attractive model for others in their conduct, speech, and lifestyle (the fruit of the Spirit)

E. Satanic strategy to abort: substitute ministry activity and/or hard work and industry for godliness and Christlikeness

F. Key steps:

1. Abide in Christ.

2. Discipline for godliness.

3. Pursue holiness in all.

G. Results: powerful Christlike example provided for others to follow

III. Competence

A. Definition: Respond in the power of the Spirit with excellence in carrying out their appointed tasks and ministry.

B. Key Scriptures to keep in mind: 2 Tim. 2:15; 2 Tim. 3:16-17; Rom. 15:14; 1 Cor. 12

C. Critical concept: By the power of the Spirit – God's leader operates in the gifting and anointing of the Holy Spirit.

D. Central elements:

1. Endowments and gifts from the Spirit

2. Sound discipling from an able mentor

3. Skill in the spiritual disciplines

4. Ability in the Word

5. Capable to evangelize, follow up, and disciple new converts

6. Strategic in the use of resources and people to accomplish God's task

E. Satanic strategy to abort: function on natural gifting and personal ingenuity rather than on the Spirit's leading and gifting

F. Key steps:

1. Discover the Spirit's gifts.

2. Receive excellent training.

3. Hone your performance.

G. Results: dynamic working of the Holy Spirit

IV. Community

A. Definition: regards multiplying disciples in the body of Christ as the primary role of ministry

B. Key Scriptures to keep in mind: Eph. 4:9-15; 1 Cor. 12:1-27

C. Critical concept: For the growth of the Church – God's leader uses all of his or her resources to equip and empower the body of Christ for her goal and task.

D. Central elements:
    1. Genuine love for and desire to serve God's people
    2. Disciples faithful individuals
    3. Facilitates growth in small groups
    4. Pastors and equips believers in the congregation
    5. Nurtures associations, networks among Christians and churches
    6. Advances new movements among God's people locally
E. Satanic strategy to abort: exalts tasks and activities above equipping the saint and developing Christian community
F. Key steps:
    1. Embrace the Church of God.
    2. Learn leadership's contexts.
    3. Equip concentrically.
G. Results: multiplying disciples in the Church

Discipling the Faithful:
Establishing Leaders for the Urban Church[2]

Rev. Dr. Don L. Davis

	Commission	Character	Competence	Community
Definition	Recognizes *the call of God* and replies with prompt obedience to his lordship and leading	Reflects *the character of Christ* in his/her personal convictions, conduct, and lifestyle	Responds in *the power of the Spirit* with excellence in carrying out their appointed tasks and ministry	Regards multiplying disciples in *the body of Christ* as the primary role of ministry
Key Scripture	2 Tim. 1.6-14; 1 Tim. 4.14; Acts 1.8; Matt. 28.18-20	John 15.4-5; 2 Tim. 2.2; 1 Cor. 4.2; Gal. 5.16-23	2 Tim. 2.15; 3.16-17; Rom. 15.14; 1 Cor. 12	Eph. 4.9-15; 1 Cor. 12.1-27
Critical Concept	The Authority of **God**: God's leader acts on God's recognized call and authority, acknowledged by the saints and God's leaders	The Humility of **Christ**: God's leader demonstrates the mind and lifestyle of Christ in his or her actions and relationships	The Power of the **Spirit**: God's leader operates in the gifting and anointing of the Holy Spirit	The Growth of the **Church**: God's leader uses all of his or her resources to equip and empower the body of Christ for his/her goal and task
Central Elements	A clear call from God Authentic testimony before God and others Deep sense of personal conviction based on Scripture Personal burden for a particular task or people Confirmation by leaders and the body	Passion for Christlikeness Radical lifestyle for the Kingdom Serious pursuit of holiness Discipline in the personal life Fulfills role-relationships and bond-slave of Jesus Christ Provides an attractive model for others in their conduct, speech, and lifestyle (the fruit of the Spirit)	Endowments and gifts from the Spirit Sound discipling from an able mentor Skill in the spiritual disciplines Ability in the Word Able to evangelize, follow up, and disciple new converts Strategic in the use of resources and people to accomplish God's task	Genuine love for and desire to serve God's people Disciples faithful individuals Facilitates growth in small groups Pastors and equips believers in the congregation Nurtures associations and networks among Christians and churches Advances new movements among God's people locally
Satanic Strategy to Abort	Operates on the basis of personality or position rather than on God's appointed call and ongoing authority	Substitutes ministry activity and/or hard work and industry for godliness and Christlikeness	Functions on natural gifting and personal ingenuity rather than on the Spirit's leading and gifting	Exalts tasks and activities above equipping the saints and developing Christian community
Key Steps	Identify God's call Discover your burden Be confirmed by leaders	Abide in Christ Discipline for godliness Pursue holiness in all	Discover the Spirit's gifts Receive excellent training Hone your performance	Embrace God's Church Learn leadership's contexts Equip concentrically
Results	Deep confidence in God arising from God's call	Powerful Christlike example provided for others to follow	Dynamic working of the Holy Spirit	Multiplying disciples in the Church

[2] *Mere Missions*, p. 215.

Seminar 9
Creating Pathways for Multiplication
Rev. Ted Smith

Creating Pathways for Multiplication

We know it may be difficult to think of multiplication while struggling to PLANT your first church. However, as Scripture suggests, healthy things grow.[1] Jesus intended that the little band of disciples gathered in the upper room (Acts 1:13) would change the world through the gospel. Indeed, it was said of early church leaders like Paul and his companions that they had "turned (their) world upside down" (Acts 17:6). The global mandate of the gospel was made clear by our Lord in all the great commission texts of the gospels (Matt. 28:18-10, for example). Amid planting your first church, your team should give ample consideration and wrestle through answering a fundamental question, "How will we multiply?"

In this section, we will explore a few models of multiplication with the goal of encouraging your team to discern your unique pathway toward reproduction even before planting your first church. All models discussed here, and other models of multiplication, require intentionality on the part of a church plant team to build multiplication into the DNA of their church.

It should be noted that multiplication is seldom accidental. Beyond the distractions of the enemy, a host of barriers will stand against your team as you move toward multiplication. One key hurdle to multiplication will be the time and attention your team gives or chooses not to give to the idea of multiplication.

To be clear, church planting is a demanding enterprise in every aspect of the word. Church plant teams will need to be able to

---

[1] Biblical texts like Mark 4:26-32 and 1 Corinthians 3:6 underscore the metaphor.

focus on the task at hand while keeping multiplication as a core principle along the way. Failure to keep multiplication at the forefront of the team's mind will present many challenges.

Church plant teams who are solely focused on planting one church will find it difficult to transition that church to next generation pastoral leadership when the time comes to multiply. Without intentionality toward multiplication the church plant team will struggle with the idea of losing valuable team members they have invested so much time to develop. They may resist sending their very best leaders out to plant other churches as doing so might detract from the newly planted church's effectiveness and capacity. This often leads to churches sending less than their very best to plant a daughter church. Certainly, a church laser focused on and stuck in one-church thinking will never find the required space and time to pray, plan, and tackle the challenges of developing a church planting movement from their church plant considering the strains of leading the one church. All of this to say, a church plant team must work diligently to keep multiplication at the center of their hearts.

We offer various models below, as we know there is no "one size fits all" model appropriate for all contexts. In all things, contextualization is key. That said, it is imperative that all churches begin with multiplication in mind regardless of the model. Church plant teams who understand multiplication as their end game will handle the process of planting their first church differently and hold their plans more loosely. A church plant team that has clarity going into their first church plant that the day will come when in some way they will release their "baby" will be freed up to operate with greater openness, creativity, flexibility, agility, and wisdom when the time comes to do so.

Models (Pathways) for Multiplication

I. Transition leadership to qualified leaders and go PLANT elsewhere.

This missionary model of church planting, the model World Impact has used through the years, envisions a church plant team planting a church knowing that they would not serve as long-term shepherds of a church which they planted. The goal of this model is to raise up local (indigenous) leaders from the community, equip them for pastoral leadership, and entrust the work to them through a formal process culminated in a commissioning service. Then the missionary team would go to their next target community and repeat the process. This approach is clearly reflected in World Impact's previous church planting resources, to date, which were developed for World Impact staff who served as largely cross-culturally missionaries to the inner-cities of America.

II. Be a Sending Church: Develop and Send Out Church Plant Teams

In this model, the church plant team plants a church with the vision to be a sending church. From inception, the church is formed with the intent to raise up and send out church plant teams, from the planted church, who will plant daughter churches. Regardless of the expression of the church that is planted, all churches should be sending churches (Acts 13:1-3) to advance the Kingdom of God in their context by releasing their very best leaders to go and PLANT new churches.

We would highly recommend that the church plant teams that you intend to send out go through an Evangel School in formal preparation toward planting their church. You can certainly send your future church plant teams through an Evangel School run by any of our Certified Evangel Deans in-person or online. However, if you intend to pursue a robust multiplication effort in which you send out multiple teams, you might want to prayerfully consider becoming a World Impact partner and running our Evangel School in your context as discussed in the "Create a Church Planting Movement" covered last in this discussion.

III. Collaborate with Other Church Planting Networks

As there are multiple church planting networks with an interest in church planting partnerships with church planters, especially those seeking to plant in urban areas, you may want to explore collaborating with multiple church planting networks in your area. You and your team will of course need to prayerfully discern which church planting networks align with your context and vision for multiplication. As this is Kingdom work, we encourage you to explore your options for collaboration with any church planting networks of like-minded hearts.

IV. Create a Church Planting Movement

Although there are many church planting networks with an interest in collaborating with church planters, some church plant teams who attend an Evangel School do so with a desire to not only develop a model for planting one church but with a view to developing a new church planting movement. If this is your interest, please note that World Impact offers the Evangel School – Dean Training designed to equip, commission, and certify leaders to offer our Evangel Schools in their context toward developing new church planting movements. If you would like more information about World Impact's Evangel

Dean Training, ask your Evangel Coach for more information and they will guide you through discerning the opportunity.

As movements are fluid, organic, and usually emerge spontaneously by people with a like-minded heart and vision which spread rapidly, it may feel forced to talk about developing a movement. However, there is nothing wrong headed about thinking through strategies and developing a plan toward launching a church planting movement, especially considering the Lord's heart that the church would expand to the ends of the earth. Said another way, all church planting movements originate from the Great Commission of our Lord.[2] Therefore, all church planting movements are branches of His singular movement and for His glory.

All of this to say, regardless of your preferred pathway give prayerful, thorough, and intentional time as a church plant team to determine your vision for multiplication and begin with that end in mind. Without intentionality, multiplication will more than likely fall through the cracks and to the bottom of your priority list. Toward that end, the tasks of identifying, equipping, and empowering leaders to plant churches as the Lord leads are essential. Building a vision for multiplication in the DNA of your church will assist you in seeing every leader in your church as a potential church plant team member and assist them in seeing the possibility that they could also be used of the Lord to serve in new church planting efforts.

---

2   See Matthew 28:18-20.

PLA(NT)

Team Exercises: Nurture and Transition

Team Exercise 8
Nurture: Mature the Church

Team Exercise 9
Transition: Multiplication Strategy

Exercise 8
Nurture: Mature the Church[1]

Your team will need to develop a strategy and plan for nurturing members and developing leaders to function in their spiritual gifts establishing a solid infrastructure.

Instructions

Discuss the following questions as a team and document your answers.

1. How will you train people to lead the church through individual and group discipleship?

2. Are there any tools or methods you will use to help people discover their gifts and talents God has given them for the church?

3. How will you assign responsibility to the faithful?

4. How will you encourage believers to exercise their gifts in the church?

5. How will you go about training a gifted, but undeveloped leader?

6. What characteristics are you looking for in potential leaders?

7. What characteristics are red flags that should give you caution?

8. What will serve as your standard for new church leadership?

9. How will you empower and equip women and men for church leadership?

---

1 Adapted from an Evangel School exercise in *Ripe for Harvest*, pp. 402-405.

10. What will be your ordination process for new pastors and shepherds (elders)?

Develop and document your goals for the next 6-12 months based on your discussions. Make sure your goals are measurable, include specific due dates, and indicate the people who will be responsible for the goal. It is okay to postpone a decision until after the Evangel School as long as you establish a goal and date by which a decision needs to be made.

Exercise 9
Transition: Multiplication Strategy[1]

Your team will need a clear vision, strategy, and plan for multiplication.

Instructions

Discuss the following questions as a team and document your answers.

1. How will you identify, acknowledge, and train emerging leaders in the church?

2. How will you equip and commission faithful leaders to be deacons, elders, and pastors?

3. What will be the signs that your church is ready to birth a daughter church?

4. What needs to be in place for the church to be self-governing, self-supporting, and part of an association of like-minded churches?

5. How will you transition initial leadership roles to a broader team?

6. What roles will you be looking to intentionally transition to new team members as they are developed?

7. How will you operate faithfully as a member church in an association or denomination of other local assemblies, for the purpose of fellowship, support, and joint-ministry activity?

8. What model of multiplication will your church pursue?

---

1 Adapted from an Evangel School exercise in *Ripe for Harvest*, pp. 416-420.

9. How will you keep multiplication at the core of your church planting efforts?

10. Do you have a strategy for how your church will plant daughter churches?

Develop and document your goals for the next 6-12 months based on your discussions. Make sure your goals are measurable, include specific due dates, and indicate the people who will be responsible for the goal. It is okay to postpone a decision until after the Evangel School as long as you establish a goal and date by which a decision needs to be made.

PLANT

SESSION 4: BRINGING IT ALL TOGETHER

In this session, we will discuss the importance of review, how to create your unique PLANT strategy, and the need to adapt to win in church planting efforts.

Seminar 10
Using Wisdom in Ministry

Seminar 11
Creating Your Strategy

Seminar 12
Adapt to Win

Seminar 10
Using Wisdom in Ministry[1]

As you engage in the rigors of church planting you will find yourself caught up in many activities which, if you are not careful, will create a chaotic and consuming sense of busyness. Learning to manage your time well, prioritizing what needs to be done over what could be done, and applying wisdom in ministry will serve you well and keep you on track. Toward this end, one of the most helpful tools you will need in church planting is a formal process for evaluating your efforts. As subjectivity and feelings are poor measures of effectiveness, wise church planters will implement an objective process of assessing their progress. The following outline introduces and describes the need and value of the PWR (prepare, work, and review) process that will help you and your team evaluate your effectiveness.

How Can We Fulfill God's Purpose? Using Wisdom in Ministry

The Dialectic: Wisdom is choosing what is best between viable truths.

Eph. 5:15-17 (ESV) – Look carefully then how you walk, not as unwise but as wise, making the best use of the time, because the days are evil. Therefore do not be foolish, but understand what the will of the Lord is.

Prov. 24:3-6 (ESV) – By wisdom a house is built, and by understanding it is established; by knowledge the rooms are filled with all precious and pleasant riches. A wise man is full of strength, and a man of knowledge enhances his might, [6] for by

---

1 Adapted from seminars by Rev. Don Allsman in *Ripe for Harvest*, pp. 65-76, 457-460.

wise guidance you can wage your war, and in abundance of counselors there is victory.

Benefits of Using Wisdom in Ministry Tasks

- Clear vision helps everyone clearly see *if the team is doing well* or not.

- Clear direction *minimizes confusion* giving a sense of confidence and hope.

- Everyone knows *their assignment*.

- People can decide if they want to stay and *help fulfill the vision* or move on to something else. You do not want people on your team who are not supporting the vision. If they stay they will either become inactive or will cause problems.

- *Wasteful activities* are minimized (stay focused on vision, not opportunities).

- An environment is created where you can say *"no" to opportunities* that do not contribute to the vision.

- Opportunities that contribute to the vision *can be anticipated* and recognized quickly. Nehemiah was ready when the opportunity arose to explain his vision to the king.

- Clarity and direction *minimizes hurting or discouraging the troops*. Soldiers die from lack of clarity and direction.

- Wisdom demands a balance between *vision (faith) and reality (prudence)*.

- Clear direction inspires people and sets them *free to innovate*.

- It provides the tools to be pro-active, *minimizing becoming a "victim of circumstances."*

- The principles can be applied to *many areas of the team's activities*. Developing a habit of using wisdom will make every activity, large or small, more effective.

Barriers to Using Wisdom in Ministry Tasks

"... we are not unaware of his schemes" (2 Cor. 2:11)

- **"We've never done it that way before."** God has no use for traditions that block his progress. Just because it has been done a certain way does not indicate it remains a wise option (Acts 10).

- **"We're doing fine."** Apparent (or real) success can keep you from greater fruitfulness (John 15:2).

- **"Being organized doesn't allow for the leading of the Holy Spirit."** God had a plan and is working his plan through us. We should not be ashamed to have a plan and work that plan.

- **"It doesn't matter what we do – God will bless it. We will face it when we come to it."** While there are some things that are better left later, sometimes this attitude reflects a lack of discipline.

- **"We can do it" rather than "we should do it."** Basing decisions on emotion, expediency, or available resources.

- **Fatigue.** "Fatigue makes cowards of us all." When we get tired, we are more resistant to new ideas and anything which will tap our already-low resources. This resistance can result in missed opportunities.

- **Fear of failure, fear of change, fear of losing supporters**

  ~ Mediocrity is preferable because it is safer.

  ~ Risk brings the prospect of personal failure and humiliation ("For God gave us a spirit not of fear but of power and love and self-control," 2 Tim. 1:7).

  ~ Natural to dread change, but we are constantly being transformed (Rom. 12:2; 2 Cor. 3:18).

  ~ Flexibility (openness to change) is critical to exercising wisdom (God does things we don't expect).

  ~ Wisdom may dictate action resulting in controversy, but if it is in the best interest of the vision, you must act courageously and sensitively.

- **Experience.** "I've been here a long time and I know what's been going on. I've been in this community for twelve years and I know this isn't going to work."

Session 4: Bringing It All Together • 95

Process that addresses barriers and benefits, and is both deliberate and emergent:

- Deliberate: Decide now, before it's too late.
- Emergent: Face when it comes.

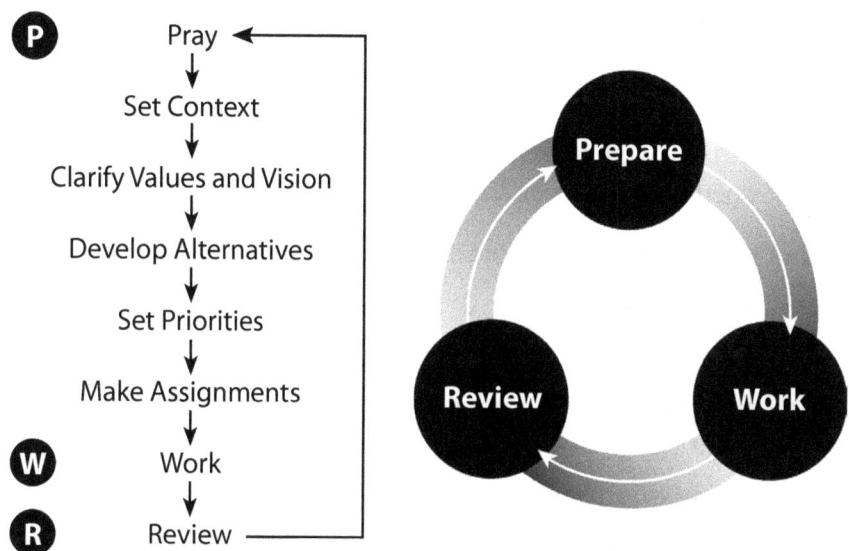

PWR

PREPARE

- *Pray* (Discover his plan.)
- *Set context* (God is God of history.)
- *Clarify the values and vision.*
- *Develop alternatives* (Don't go with the first, most obvious answer.)
- *Set priorities* (Don't just try all the alternatives.)
- *Make assignments* (Don't leave people guessing about the specifics of their assignment.)

WORK (Stop talking and start doing.)

- Be bold; innovate.
- Friction: things seldom go as planned.
- Better to execute a poor plan than poorly execute a great plan.
- *Be creative* (Matt. 25:14-30).
- Two extremes: rigidity and lack of discipline.

REVIEW (Don't assume what you did was effective.)

- Make half-time adjustments (Sanballat, Cornelius, Gideon, Macedonian vision).
- Check the fruit (John 15:2).
- "The most important part of any mission is the debrief."
- *Be reflective.* "Poverty and disgrace come to him who ignores instruction, but whoever heeds reproof is honored. . . . Whoever ignores instruction despises himself, but he who listens to reproof gains intelligence" (Prov. 13:18; 15:32).
- Celebrate!

What Is PWR?

You will spend much time in preparation, but don't be deceived. No formula or good plan will plant a church; not an analytic process.

PWR Is About	PWR Is Not About
Adapting	Being organized
Wisdom (wisely pursuing vision)	Goals
Adjustment	Checking off tasks
Learning	Planning
Contribution to vision	Calculated analysis
Fruit checking (John 15:2)	Bean counting
Dreaming and scheming	Paperwork
"Rapid assessment and adaptation to a complex and rapidly changing environment that you can't control" (John Boyd, OODA Loop)	Being linear
Prepare, Work, Review	Pain Without Reward

Applications for PWR

Dimensions: leading a choir, leading a worship service, leading a cell group, elder meetings, worship services, retreats, evangelistic events.

PWR represents biblical principles of wisdom.

Victory is found when:

There is wise preparation
>   . . . creatively executed under the guidance of the Holy Spirit
>   . . . and rigorously reviewed.

The Importance of Review

The real payoff from **PWR** is not in the first cycle, despite its many benefits.

Some percentage of your plans will not work.

The real value of **PWR** is the ability to adapt. Once you've tried something and then learned from the **PW**, the **WR** kicks in and you can become effective.

It is not the *Preparation* that is key, it is the *Review*.

But you cannot *Review* without *Work*. *Work* without *Preparation* is folly.

I. A Good Sports Team Makes Effective Half-time Adjustments.

II. Process of Review

    A. Review vision statement.

    B. Review objectives, goals, assignments.

    C. Review results.

    D. Assess if results were desired.

E. Questions

   1. What went well?

   2. What didn't go well?

   3. What should be abandoned?

   4. What should be added or modified?

III. Enter the Prepare Stage Again.

   A. New objectives, goals, and assignments

   B. Brainstorming and prioritizing

IV. Celebrate.

V. Keep Setbacks in Perspective.

Finally, be strong in the Lord and in the strength of his might. Put on the whole armor of God, that you may be able to stand against the schemes of the devil.... Obey your leaders and submit to them, for they are keeping watch over your souls, as those who will have to give an account.... Count it all joy, my brothers, when you meet trials of various kinds, for you know that the testing of your faith produces steadfastness. And let steadfastness have its full effect, that you may be perfect and complete, lacking in nothing.

~ Ephesians 6.10-11; Hebrews 13.17a; James 1.2-4

Seminar 11
Creating Your Strategy

As noted in previous seminars, it is of utmost importance that your team apply the PLANT principles of the Evangel School to the context of the community your church will serve and to the vision God has given you.

In this seminar, we will review the PLANT phases of Evangel as applied by World Impact in its church planting efforts. Note that this is offered as an example and descriptive of a contextual strategy. The chart below is not intended to be prescriptive to you and your context. Your task is to take the principles and phases of Evangel and draft your unique strategy.

In addition, we will introduce and explain the role of the Evangel Charter. In practical terms, the charter will be used as a coaching document. The charter will summarize your strategic plan and guide your team. Your Evangel Field Coach will utilize the charter as a guide in coaching sessions to review your progress, celebrate victories, address challenges, and suggest necessary course adjustments along the way as needed. In simple terms, the charter is your strategic plan. Therefore, teams should give much prayerful consideration to ensure that the charter clearly represents their goals and strategies.

Overview of Exercise Phases for World Impact's Evangel School of Urban Church Planting[1]

	Definition and Purpose	As Relates to Parent-Child Metaphor
Prepare *Be the Church*	**Definition** Forming a team of called members who ready themselves to plant a church under the Holy Spirit's guidance **Purpose** Seek God regarding the target population and community, the formation of your church plant team, organizing strategic intercession for the community, and doing research on its needs and opportunities	Decision and Conception
Launch *Expand the Church*	**Definition** Penetrating the selected community by conducting evangelistic events among the target population **Purpose** Mobilize team and recruit volunteers to conduct ongoing evangelistic events and holistic outreach to win associates and neighbors to Christ	Prenatal Care
Assemble *Establish the Church*	**Definition** Gathering the cells of converts together to form a local assembly of believers, announcing the new church to the neighbors in the community **Purpose** Form cell groups, Bible studies, or home fellowships for follow-up, continued evangelism, and ongoing growth toward public birth of the church	Childbirth
Nurture *Mature the Church*	**Definition** Nurturing member and leadership discipleship, enabling members to function in their spiritual gifts, and establishing solid infrastructure within the Christian assembly **Purpose** Develop individual and group discipleship by filling key roles in the body based on burden and gifting of members	Growth and Parenting
Transition *Multiply the Church*	**Definition** Empowering the church for independence by equipping leaders for autonomy, transferring authority, and creating structures for financial independence **Purpose** Commission members and elders, install pastor, and foster church associations	Maturity to Adulthood

---

1   *Ripe for Harvest*, pp. 462-463.

Question Focus During Dialogue	Cardinal Virtue and Critical Vices	Bottom Line
Questions about: • preparing your team • the target community • strategic prayer initiatives • demographic studies	**Virtue** Openness to the Lord **Vices** Presumption and "paralysis of analysis"	Cultivate a period of listening and reflecting
Questions about: • character and number of evangelistic events • communication and advertisement of events • recruiting and coordinating volunteers • identity and name of the outreach	**Virtue** Courage to engage the community **Vices** Intimidation and haughtiness	Initiate your engagement with boldness and confidence
Questions about: • follow-up and incorporation of new believers • make-up of small group life • the character of public worship • initial church structures and procedures • initial body life and growth • cultural friendliness of the church	**Virtue** Wisdom to discern God's timing **Vices** Impatience and cowardice	Celebrate the announcement of your body with joy
Questions about: • discipling individuals and leaders • helping members identify gifts and burdens (teams) • credentials for leadership • church order, government, discipline	**Virtue** Focus upon the faithful core **Vices** Neglect and micro-management	Concentrate on investing in the faithful
Questions about: • incorporation • affiliations and associations • transferring leadership • missionary transition • ongoing reproduction	**Virtue** Dependence on the Spirit's ability **Vices** Paternalism and quick release	Pass the baton with confidence in the Spirit's continued working

Bringing It All Together[1]

I. What is a charter?

A. It is a written record of the intentions of the church plant team.

B. It provides means of accountability to leadership.

C. It provides clarity of action so the team can continue if there are changes in team personnel.

D. It provides a limited amount of time to complete the task.

II. Why is it important?

A. Church plant teams tend to either take too long without results or get discouraged and want to quit too early. Charters minimize quitting and languishing by giving time frames.

B. Church plant teams need accountability on a periodic basis but not micro-management. Charters free up the team to be creative within their stated guidelines so there isn't excessive oversight that would hinder the effort. Charters also provide a written statement of goals and objectives so there can be specific checkpoints providing accountability to the stated plan.

C. Charters provide a written plan for the next year that helps the team stay on course, minimizing wasted efforts.

D. If there are multiple church plants occurring in an area, charters help scope out the target areas so new efforts are not causing a duplication of effort.

---

1 *Ripe for Harvest*, pp. 464-466.

Seminar 12
Adapt to Win[1]

Throughout this resource much has been offered to underscore the value of the careful, thoughtful, and prayerful planning needed for church planting. As anyone who has ever planned anything can attest, plans are great until they are not. We recognize that you will face many unforeseen challenges, obstacles, and barriers along with some surprisingly joyful circumstances as you plant that will require adjustments to your plan.

A key virtue of all church planters and their teams is flexibility. We know that inevitably you will need to adapt your plans as you move forward. Your team will need to operate in the spirit of adaptation and make many course corrections as you carry out the vision the Lord has given you. The following outline is offered to help your team prepare for the road ahead. How your team responds to difficulties and adapts to challenges will determine your success.

In order to adapt to win, we must recognize the axioms of adaptation:

I. The Inevitability of Trouble: Things Mess Up

This world is a fallen world, and is subject to satanic oppression, attack, and subversion.

   A. All your church planting is undertaken behind enemy lines.

      1. The *world* is the external enemy, distracting you from your calling and mission, 1 John 2:15-17.

---

[1] Adapted from a seminar by Rev. Dr. Don L. Davis in *Ripe for Harvest*, pp. 443-449.

2. The *flesh* is the traitor within, sabotaging your best intentions and commitments, Gal. 5:16-24.

3. The *devil* is the god of this world, accusing, tempting, and undermining all you seek to do for Christ, Eph. 6:10-12.

B. The difficulties you face will be multiple, constant, mind-boggling, and exhausting (John 15:18-21; James 1:2-3; 1 Pet. 1:6-7; 5:8-9).

C. Stuff that normally happens in an effective church planting ministry:

1. You are forced to operate understaffed and under-planned.

2. Undelegated work falls in your lap.

3. Trusted team members quit or fight.

4. Your plans go completely south.

5. You lack the proper equipment.

6. The ragged equipment you have gives up the ghost.

7. You run out of money, time, and energy.

8. You or other trusted workers get sick, at the absolutely wrong time.

9. You lose support, financially, spiritually, personally.

10. Your students, mentors, volunteers quit.

11. You become disillusioned and quit!

> Human progress is neither automatic nor inevitable.... Every step toward the goal of justice requires sacrifice, suffering, and struggle; the tireless exertions and passionate concern of dedicated individuals.
>
> ~ Martin Luther King, Jr.

    D. To adapt is to fight zealously to complete your mission: adaptation demands heavenly armor.

        1. You are *exposed*: strap your armor on, Eph. 6:13.

        2. Your enemy is *determined*: don't be ignorant of his schemes, 2 Cor. 2:11.

        3. Your innovation is *demanded*: you must adapt or lose (or die!), Gal. 5:1.

Your question: *How does our church plant team identify and make provision for the opposition you will face ahead?*

II. The Certainty of Change: Nothing in Your Ministry Theater Will Remain Stable or Constant.

No matter how much we pray and prepare, we will never be able to know all the changes, obstacles, and challenges ahead. Therefore, we ought to always take our next steps boldly, and yet be ready for the contingencies we'll face in the future.

    A. Defuse drama by anticipating and accepting it.

        1. Don't fall apart in the midst of difficulty, innovate!, Eph. 3:20-21.

        2. Welcome trial as an opportunity to re-calibrate your situation: nothing is too hard for the Lord, Jer. 32:17.

3. Don't marvel when you face trials; remember, all your fellow workers are facing the same difficulties and challenges, too, 1 Pet. 5:9.

B. Planning is important, but plans will always need updating.

1. Planning produces freshness, but plans will often grow stale.

2. Planning forces us to respect the current situation (i.e., "to look again, to consider anew), while allegiance to old plans may or may not now be relevant.

3. Planning opens you up to dialogue, but commitment to old plans may freeze you into commitments in pursuing bad directions.

C. Flexibility ensures successful execution

1. Walk in the Spirit: let everything you do be informed by an openness to the Spirit's word and prompting, Gal. 5:16.

2. Quench not the Spirit: do not refuse the Holy Spirit's instruction and leading through the Word, through others, and through circumstances, 1 Thess. 5:19.

3. Be led by the Spirit: act on what the Holy Spirit tells you, promptly and completely, Rom. 8:14.

Your question: *Is our church plant team prepared for the changes ahead?*

III. The Necessity of Support: In Order to Adapt, We Must Recruit and Coordinate Gifted Team Members.

Talent wins games, but teamwork and intelligence wins championships.

~ Michael Jordan

Problems in ministry usually are complex, multi-layered, and come in bunches. Therefore, we will often require other team members to contribute to solutions to ensure our ability to attain our objectives.

A. Ministry challenges are too complex for any one individual.

Mark 3:14 (ESV) – And he appointed twelve (whom he also named apostles) so that they might be with him and he might send them out to preach.

1. Your church difficulties will quickly outweigh your individual strength and experience.

2. Leverage the gifts of your team members for maximum success.

3. Church leadership development demands the ability to identify and coordinate gifted people who can help you attain your training mission.

B. Even gifted teams face dysfunction and disunity.

Phil 4:2-3 – I entreat Euodia and I entreat Syntyche to agree in the Lord. Yes, I ask you also, true companion, help these women, who have labored side by side with me in the gospel together with Clement and the rest of my fellow workers, whose names are in the book of life.

1. They fight: Paul and Barnabas, Acts 15:36-40.
2. They fail: John Mark, Acts 13:13.
3. They quit: Demas, 2 Tim. 4:10.

C. Build your ministry around solid, effective team members.

Rom. 12:4-6 – For as in one body we have many members, and the members do not all have the same function, so we, though many, are one body in Christ, and individually members one of another. Having gifts that differ according to the grace given to us, let us use them: if prophecy, in proportion to our faith.

1. Spend time daily praying for your entire team network, Jer. 33:3.
2. Actively recruit the best workers to join your enterprise, 2 Tim. 2:2.
3. Delegate authority to faithful team members.

Your question: *Is our church plant recruiting, equipping, and releasing the best team members we can find to support your church plant strategy?*

The Final Acclamation

> Trust in the LORD with all your heart, and do not lean on your own understanding. In all your ways acknowledge him, and he will make straight your paths.
>
> ~ Proverbs 3:5-6 (ESV)

PLANT

TEAM EXERCISES: BRINGING IT ALL TOGETHER

Team Exercise 10
Creating a Church Planting Calendar

Team Exercise 11
Completing Your Evangel Charter

Exercise Supplement
Sample Evangel Charter

Exercise 10
Creating a Church Planting Calendar[1]

Your team will need to develop a strategic plan to plant or re-plant a church.

Instructions

Based on the goals you identified while working through team exercises with your Evangel Coach, develop a team calendar for the next 12 months.

    A. Create a visual schedule on a table using post-it notes and butcher paper.

        1. At the top of the table, place a card for each month of the next 12 months, left to right.

Week	MAY	JUNE	JULY	AUG	SEPT	OCT
1						
2						
3						
4						
5						

        2. Write down each goal for the next 12 months only on a post-it note with:

            a. What is to be completed

            b. Finish date (and start date if relevant)

            c. Who is responsible to see it gets done

---

1 Adapted from an Evangel School exercise in *Ripe for Harvest*, pp. 464-466.

> Note: Some teams color code by person responsible, others by PLANT phase, others no color coding at all.

   3. Place each note in the month where it belongs.
   4. See if you want to make any adjustments to any part of the plan you have already made.
      a. Postpone an action
      b. Move an action to an earlier or later date
      c. Add a new idea
      d. Get rid of an idea
   5. Tape the notes to the paper. Roll up the paper to take it home where it can be re-created.
B. Summarize the results on the charter form.
   1. Write out the vision statement and all the other information requested on the form.
   2. The requested length of charter is generally the date from your vision statement. But in some rare cases, it could be shorter if you want to have a formal charter review at an earlier date.
   3. Note: If you decide to add a team member at a later date, it is highly recommended that you take the person through a formal process of commitment to the team and your vision. Other teams have suffered when members are added without the thorough understanding of, and commitment to, the team's vision and goals.
   4. Write down your key goals.

1. Work as a team to create your 12-month calendar. Your calendar should have monthly and quarterly goals.

2. Make sure your goals are measurable, with due dates, and the people responsible to see that it gets done to support your decisions.

3. Brainstorming is good, but you will need to apply wisdom to prioritize what needs to be done and what can wait.

Exercise 11
Completing Your Evangel Charter[1]

Your team will need to complete an Evangel Charter which will serve as your strategic plan and coaching agreement with your Evangel Field Coach by pulling together the information and goals from previous sessions and team exercises.

Instructions

To prepare to complete the Charter your team will need to be able to provide the following:

1. Discuss the following items toward completing your Evangel Charter

    - Sending Authority/Denomination/Affiliation/Network
    - Church Plant Name
    - Church Plant Team Leader
    - Church Plant Team Leader Email
    - Church Plant Team Leader Cell
    - Primary Team Members and Length of Commitment (at least three people)
    - Target Area (city, state, and community)
    - Ethnicity and/or Unreached People Group(s)
    - Unengaged and Unreached People Group (if applicable)
    - Church Vision and Church Values

---

1   Adapted from an Evangel School exercise in *Ripe for Harvest*, pp. 464-466.

- Church Expression
- Key Goals for the next 12 months (Be specific, list your largest goals and due dates)
- Length of Charter Requested: (typically one year)
- Field Coach Name, Email, and Cell
- Proposed times to Meet with Field Coach (at least quarterly)
- Scheduled time of Formal Evaluation (PWR, at least three times per year)
- Signatures (team leader, Evangel Field Coach, and Evangel Dean)

2. Once you have the information above complete your Evangel Charter document.

Note: Again, should you decide to add a team member later, it is highly recommended that you take the person through a formal process of commitment to the team and your vision. Other teams have suffered when members are added without a thorough understanding of, and commitment to, the team's vision and goals.

Exercise Supplement
Sample Evangel Charter

Evangel School of Urban Church Planting
Church Plant Charter Form

Sending Authority/Denomination/Affiliation/Network:
Fairview Community Church

Church Plant Name: Greendale Community Church

Church Plant Team Leader: Lead Church Planter Person

Church Plant Team Leader Email: planter@madeupdomain.com

Church Plant Team Leader Cell: (555) 555-5555

Primary Team Members and Length of Commitment:
1. Team member 1 (5 years)
2. Team member 2 (3 years)
3. Team member 3 (2 years)
4. Team member 4 (1 year)

Target Area: Greendale, WI

Ethnicity and/or Unreached People Group(s): The multicultural community of Greendale

Unengaged and Unreached People Group (if applicable): N/A

Church Vision:
To be a church that reaches the Greendale community with the gospel of Jesus Christ.

Church Values:
Teaching God's Word, Reaching out to the community, Fellowship

Church Expression (Check one or all that apply):
- ☐ Small (House) Church [approximately 20-50]
- ☒ Community Church [approximately 50-150]
- ☐ Hub (Mother) Church [200+]

Key Goals for the next 12 months:

- Establish regular Team meetings schedule by April 1
- Complete neighborhood demographic data by April 15
- Research community service organizations in the neighborhood by May 1
- Visit local service organizations by May 15
- Research other churches in the community June 1
- Research collaborative church events with pastors in the community by June 15
- Conduct a neighborhood survey by July 1
- Create church on board materials for potential team members July 15
- Hold 1st interest meeting with potential team members and guests by Aug 1
- On-board and train new team members by Aug 15
- Develop 3 platforms for online social media presence by Sept 1
- Create a church member profile (the ideal church member) by Sept 15
- Create church promotional material and membership class materials by Oct 1
- Conduct an evangelistic "fall Festival" community service event by Oct 31
- Follow up with contacts made "we are praying for you card" by Nov. 15
- Hold 2nd interest meeting with potential team members and guests by Dec 1
- On-board and train new team members by December 15
- Determine and secure meeting location by January 15
- Determine worship team and preaching schedule by Feb 1
- Develop worship and preaching series for the first six months by Feb 15
- Decide on follow up strategy for events and guests by March 1
- Distribute flyers in door-to-door evangelism in the neighborhood by March 15
- Full court press on social media and follow up by April 1
- Church Launch on Easter Sunday (with Easter Egg Hunt), April 20

Length of Charter Requested (typically one year): 1 year

Field Coach Name: Evangel Field Coach Person

Field Coach Email: EvangelFC@madeupdomain.com

Field Coach Cell: (555) 555-5555

Times to Meet with Field Coach:
1st Monday evening of each month – via Zoom (7:00pm-8:00pm CST)

Time of Formal Evaluation (PWR, at least three times per year):
- May 15 – via Zoom (10:00am-11:30am, CST)
- August 15 – via Zoom (10:00am-11:30am, CST)
- November 15 – via Zoom (10:00am-11:30am, CST)
- March 15 – via Zoom (10:00am-11:30am, CST)

Monthly team meetings:
We will meet on the first and third Sunday of every month after service for team discussion and PWR time.

Signatures (type or sign your name):

Church Plant Team Leader: <u>Church Planter</u>   Date: <u>March 27, 2024</u>

Evangel Field Coach: <u>Evangel Coach Person</u>   Date: <u>March 27, 2024</u>

Evangel Dean Approval: <u>Evangel Dean Person</u>   Date: <u>March 27, 2024</u>

Afterword
Rev. Ted Smith

Throughout this book we have noted several resources upon which our work rests. These resources are readily available to you on World Impact's Evangel Church Planting Bookshelf (worldimpact.org/cpbookshelf) in digital format as well as available for purchase via Amazon.

The following is an introduction of key texts that may be helpful as you and your team continue the work of church planting, applying the principles of the Evangel School of Urban Church Planting.

Ripe for Harvest:
A Guidebook for Planting Healthy Churches in the City

This guidebook was the original text of the Evangel School, outlining a process of church planting that respects the unique cultures, environments, communities, and situations reflected in urban America. The PLANT approach outlined provides practically wise and spiritually vital instruction to ensure that urban church planting teams will neither fail nor blunder as they seek to engage needy yet spiritually ripe unreached neighborhoods. The guidebook will guide teams through that process, with a focus on prayer, reflection, and wisdom to find God's unique call on each planter and team. Filled with devotionals, seminars, exercises, and worksheets, with dozens of graphics, diagrams, and articles, this rich resource will empower church planting teams to design a strategy that will prove empowering to them. It can enable them to draft a course that is consistent with the vision God has given them to plant a healthy, Kingdom-declaring church, and launch movements that display the justice of the Kingdom among the oppressed. We are excited about both the interest and activity of many churches and denominations to establish outposts of the Kingdom in the neediest communities in our nation. Our prayer is that this resource contributes to that vision.

Planting Churches among the City's Poor:
An Anthology of Urban Church Planting Resources, Volume One:
Theological and Missiological Perspectives for Church Planters

Volume One contains a range of materials related to the whys and wherefores of a biblical theology of mission and church planting, especially how that theology touches upon urban missions, church planting, and the development of healthy congregations and movements.

In this collection you will find our formative, seminal essay on urban church planting which served as the foundational biblical and theological piece which informed our initial forays into church planting among the poor in the city. It also includes Theological and Missiological Principles and Insights providing a treasure of resources related to urban missions, ministry among the poor and oppressed, and church planting, including biblical theologies of the Church, retrieval of the Great Tradition among churches which serve the poor, and the role of color, class, and race in making disciples in underserved communities. In addition, the resources contains material related to the theory and practice of actually planting churches among the urban poor, with a focus on the calling, character, and competencies of the church planter, that God-called, Spirit-filled individual who has been led to plant outposts of the Kingdom for Christ among the city's poorest and most vulnerable populations.

Planting Churches among the City's Poor:
An Anthology of Urban Church Planting Resources, Volume Two:
Resources and Tools for Coaches and Teams

Volume Two provides a toolkit, an asset depot containing various materials, tools, and helps to outfit the church plant coach or mentor to lead teams. Additionally, this volume contains numerous specific aids that the planter and his/her team will find invaluable as they engage in their church planting effort.

In this collection you will find a host of articles addressing the specific nature of coaching and mentoring church plant leaders and their teams, and seeks to give a broad, compelling outline of the kinds of issues, concerns, and commitments necessary for mentors to understand and do as they coach teams that plant effective churches. It also includes a collection of miscellaneous articles, graphs, documents, and information relevant to planting a church, including information about financial, state relations, leadership development, forming associations, and equipping for reproduction in church planting movements. In this section you will find abundant particular resources all meant to be helpful for planters, coaches, and associations who desire to plant healthy churches among the poor, both cross-culturally and intra-culturally.

These many helps will readily inform your thinking about the nature of planting the individual congregation, forming the structures of a healthy church planting movement, empowering leadership for reproduction, and advancing the Kingdom among the poor in the city.

Other Available Resources

On This Rock: A Church Planting Sampler

This sampler represents the training materials of World Impact, a Christian missions organization which has ministered in the inner cities of America for more than forty years (www.worldimpact.org). We are deeply committed to facilitating church-planting movements by evangelizing, equipping, and empowering the unchurched urban poor. World Impact's purpose is to honor and glorify God and to delight in him among the unchurched urban poor by knowing God and making him known. For us, the fastest, most efficient, and most powerful method to impact and transform urban poor communities is to plant healthy Christ-centered churches where the light and life of Jesus Christ is proclaimed and demonstrated for all to see. Our belief is that through the planting of healthy churches among the poor, the Holy Spirit will show his transformative power within and through the members of these neighborhoods. Our hope is that this sampler will trigger a desire for you to move from a mere taste of materials to the actual full texts which are available to you at our online store (www.tumientree.com). Hopefully, a perusal of these diverse materials will provide you with a sense of our commitment to seeing the Great Commission fulfilled among the world's urban poor, and what we believe we will need to accomplish this.

Fit to Represent: Vision for Discipleship Seminar

Are You Fit to Represent Christ and His Kingdom? The Great Commission of our Lord Jesus commands us to make disciples of all nations, i.e., among all the people groups of the families of humankind. In order to fulfill his great command, we must understand what it means to be a disciple, a follower of our Rabbi Jesus in the 21st century. The Vision for Discipleship Seminar is the Urban Ministry Institute's attempt to raise up a new generation of qualified spiritual laborers who will catch the passion to invest in others for the sake of the Church and

Christ's Kingdom. This handbook represents the text that guides the dialogues among the Seminar's participants. These spirited and challenging sessions are designed to confront the learners with the call of our Lord to be and to make disciples, to embrace a life lived for Christ and his church, and to join forces with World Impact to see revival come to the inner cities of America and the world. Let this Vision for Discipleship Seminar guidebook help you discover the process and mindset to share your life with others in such a way that real fruit will be borne for Christ—fruit that lasts.

Sacred Roots: A Primer on Retrieving the Great Tradition

The Christian faith is anchored on the person and work of Jesus of Nazareth, the Christ, whose incarnation, crucifixion, and resurrection forever changed the world. Between the years 100 and 500 C.E. those who believed in him grew from a small persecuted minority to a strong aggressive movement reaching far beyond the bounds of the Roman empire. The roots this era produced gave us our canon (the Scriptures), our worship, and our conviction (the major creeds of the Church, and the central tenets of the Faith, especially regarding the doctrine of the Trinity and Christ). This book suggests how we can renew our contemporary faith again, by rediscovering these roots, our Sacred Roots, by retrieving the Great Tradition of the Church that launched the Christian revolution.

www.ingramcontent.com/pod-product-compliance
Lightning Source LLC
Chambersburg PA
CBHW060325050426
42449CB00011B/2652